Kate Chopin's

The Awakening

Study notes for Area of Study:

Discovery

2015-2018 HSC

William Burden

A FIVE SENSES PUBLICATION

Five Senses Education Pty Ltd
2/195 Prospect Highway
Seven Hills 2147
New South Wales
Australia

First Published 2014

Burden, William
Top Notes – The Awakening
ISBN 978 -1- 74130 – 996 – 6

CONTENTS

TOP NOTES SERIES

This series has been created to assist HSC students of English in their understanding of set texts. Top Notes are easy to read, providing analysis of issues and discussion of important ideas contained in the texts.

Particular care has been taken to ensure that students are able to examine each text in the context of the module it has been allocated to.

Each text generally includes:

- Notes on the specific module
- Plot summary
- Character analysis
- Setting
- Thematic concerns
- Language studies
- Essay questions and a modelled response
- Other textual material
- Study practice questions
- Useful quotes

We have covered the areas we feel are important for students in their study of Discovery for their Area of Study. I am sure you will find these Top Notes useful in your studies of English.

Bruce Pattinson
Series Editor

AREA OF STUDY: DISCOVERY

We learn wisdom from failure much more than from success. We often discover what will do, by finding out what will not do; and probably he who never made a mistake never made a discovery.

SAMUEL SMILES

What is the Area of Study?

The Area of Study set for the 2015–18 HSC is *Discovery*. It is compulsory to study this topic as prescribed by the Board of Studies. For your studies there are no other focuses and you will need to be flexible in your approach to the area. Remember you are supposed to analyse the relationship between your texts and *Discovery*. There are no right or wrong answers in the Area of Study–it is about how you see and interpret material and engage with it.

In the Area of Study you will be analysing many texts that are related to the idea of discovery. You will analyse texts not only to investigate the ideas they present about this area but also how they deliver these ideas. This means you will be looking closely at the techniques a composer uses to represent his/her messages and shape meaning. You will also be looking at relationships between texts. Overall, you will become an expert on discovery-the different notions people have about it and the various ways composers manipulate techniques to communicate their ideas about the topic. The material in this Top Note will help you do that.

Specifically you will look at:

- A set text from the following list of fourteen texts. **You will only study one of these.**
  - *Wrack* – James Bradley
  - *The Awakening* – Kate Chopin
  - *A Short History of Nearly Everything* – Bill Bryson
  - *The Motorcycle Diaries* – Ernesto 'Che' Guevara
  - *Swallow the Air* – Tara June Winch
  - *Away* – Michael Gow
  - *Rainbow's End* – Jane Harrison
  - *Frank Hurley - The Man Who Made History* – Simon Nasht
  - *Life of Pi* – Ang Lee
  - *The Tempest* – William Shakespeare
  - *Selected Poems* – Robert Gray
  - *Selected Poems*– Rosemary Dobson
  - *Selected Poems* – Robert Frost
  - *Go Back To Where You Came From* – selected episodes – Ivan O'Mahoney
- Additional related texts of your own choosing

You must write about your set text and additional texts of your own choosing in the first English paper of the H.S.C. examination.

> *I hope that posterity will judge me kindly, not only as to the things which I have explained, but also to those which I have intentionally omitted so as to leave to others the pleasure of discovery.*
>
> **RENE DESCARTES**

WHAT DOES THE BOARD OF STUDIES REQUIRE FOR THE AREA OF STUDY?

The Board of Studies documentation says of the Area of Study: Discovery that it;

> *'requires students explore the ways in which the concept of discovery is represented in and through texts.' (p 9)*

The document English Stage 6 Prescriptions: Area of Study Electives and Texts (August 2013) notes that perceptions of discovery can encompass many things and are shaped by context.

- Students can consider discovery and rediscovery.
- The discovery may be planned or unplanned and may lead us to new worlds and values.
- Discoveries can question and challenge and lead to different conclusions.

You will also need to consider that the 'process of discovering can vary according to personal, cultural, historical and social contexts and values.'

Below is an abbreviated version of what the Board requires of students.

'In their responses and compositions students examine, question, and reflect and speculate on':

- their own experiences of discovery, personally and through texts.
- the assumptions underlying the representations of discovery.

- the effect of composers' choice of techniques.
- the ways in which your study of discovery can help you understand the world and yourself.

Think carefully about the wording that is used so that you can adopt this language for your own work.

If this is what is required by the Board of Studies we need to examine the concept of discovery carefully so we can adequately respond in these ways. I would recommend that you read the complete document which is on the Board of Studies website and can be downloaded in Word or PDF formats.

UNDERSTANDING THE AREA OF STUDY

'There is no better high than discovery'

- WILSON

What is Discovery?

The word *Discovery* seems innately connected to humanity and usually dredges up childhood images of exotic locations and intrepid explorers heading out into the jungles to discover lost tribes, great treasures or other such imaginatively wonderful thoughts. Discovery is also an emotive word that engages on a broader social context. For example we have a Discovery Channel that exists to meet a genuine need for people to absorb the unknown. This idea even extends to space where the purpose of the never-ending Star Trek series states its mission is to 'explore strange new worlds, to seek out new life and new civilisations, to boldly go where no man has gone before'.

Even the self-discovery/ self-help industry is a major one in all the nations of earth; people are willing to make great sacrifices to discover the 'truth' about themselves and the world. All this is undoubtedly true but discovery is much more than this and we will need to have a broader and more sophisticated understanding to undertake our studies of the texts set for study.

The Board of Studies has outlined in their documentation: students are required to 'explore the ways in which the concept of discovery is represented in and through texts'. (p9. *HSC Prescriptions 2015- 20 English Stage 6*). This is our first step and it indicates that we must pay particular attention to the text and its language, particularly the techniques the composer uses to engage the audience and convey the main purpose of their text.

The whole aim of this Area of Study is to examine the text closely but also relate it to the idea of discovery and decide how examining it in this way enables us to better understand both the text and the concept of *Discovery*. It is important that you formulate your own ideas about the text and attempt to develop some original and creative ideas about what you are studying.

The Board's documentation should be read in full and the annotations document should also be examined for the particular texts you are studying as this document offers insights into the way each particular text should be examined by outlining key ideas and areas for clarification.

The *Prescriptions* document states on the Area of Study that *Discovery* can be:

- something new
- a rediscovery
- sudden, unexpected

- carefully planned
- 'fresh and intensely meaningful in ways that may be emotional, creative, intellectual, physical and spiritual.' (p9)
- confronting
- provocative
- create new values
- enable speculation
- change perceptions of individuals, groups etc.

The document also suggests that discoveries and ways of discovering vary due to individual circumstance and that these discoveries can change many things about lives, communities and the world(s). Of course when we examine the concept of discovery we need to examine how 'discovering' the text itself may change us and how we view things. The text may challenge and confront and change how we see the human experience.

Students can also think about 'their own experiences of discovery' and how composer's choice of form, feature, language etc. influences their views of discovery. Examining and enjoying any text is a discovery in itself but it is what we take away from the text and apply that is the real discovery. That is not to say that every text will be enjoyed or offer a discovery. Some may not personally engage you and that is fine. This is especially so when you begin to find other related material that links to *Discovery*. Find examples of texts that link but also personally appeal to you so that you can relate empathetically with them.

Defining Discovery

'Definition is the death of discovery'

-TON SHADYAK

Now let's define discovery in a more coherent and easily understood way so we can begin our investigation at a basic level before moving into more complex analysis. Dictionary.com defines the term as:

1. The act or instance of discovering
2. Something discovered
3. In legal terms it is compulsory disclosure of evidence
4. The name of the third space shuttle.

Obviously the first three terms are more suitable but the final definition shows how pervasive the idea of discovery is and how it has influenced people over time. The search for the 'new' has driven much development over past millennia. Discoveries are always met with excitement and often trepidation as to what change they might bring.

Think historically about how people have reacted to change. It can cause great upheavals in society, with violent reactions while other changes brought through discoveries are welcomed and may save and enhance lives. Consider medical advancements, scientific developments and the ever-quickening world of the computer. Even the way I am creating this text in Evernote on an iPad would not have been possible twelve months ago. Discovery brings change and may affect different people or groups of people, even nations in various ways both positive and negative. It is pertinent now to examine some more definitions.

The word discover and its definition also sheds some light on the concept:

1. To see, get knowledge, to learn, to find, get knowledge of something previously seen or unknown.

As does the definition of the word discovering:

1. noticing or realising.

These definitions all point to the fact that realisation is the key to discovery. This realisation may come unexpectedly, occasionally or never. Someone else may have the same experience and make the discovery. The realisation may be accidental or organised, years in the planning or come as a complete surprise.

Discoveries can come in many ways and the synonyms for discovery listed below help us to understand the concept even further. They assist in defining how a discovery can arise:

Synonyms – ascertain, catch, come upon, contrive, determine, design, dig up, disclose, elicit, explore, bring to light, unearthing, ascertainment, encounter, experimentation, invention, origination, unearthing, exploration, exposure, location, perception, sensing, strike, verification

These synonyms show partly the vast array of words that our language has created around this concept and shows how important it is in the human psyche. Look also at the antonyms that show how we view not discovering things; lose, miss, pass by. We, as a race, want to discover and now we will look at some examples of discovery and examine how they can impact. It is also important to remember that discoveries do not have to be positive. You might discover you have a huge problem, an incurable illness, a strange past, an unwelcome relative or something equally bizarre. There is always a darker side to any discovery that may need to be addressed. Think about the effect of the white discoverers on indigenous populations.

Types of Discovery

Personal Discovery

'I think a spiritual journey is not so much a journey of discovery. It's a journey of recovery. It's a journey of uncovering your own inner nature. It's already there.'

BILLY CORGAN

The idea of personal discovery or self-discovery as many of the books also describe it, is a popular and pervasive concept. It is more prevelant in the developed nations of the world where people seek something more spiritual or meaningful rather than their consumer driven lives and the day to day grind of work. Many seek something more; they strive to discover something within or without, a better self, a way to live in the now or just a way to escape from reality. A huge amount of material (literature, DVDs, audiobooks etc.) has been assembled to help individuals achieve their life goals.

Individuals seek to achieve personal discovery in a variety of ways. Some examples are courses and conferences where they are led through exercises, both physical and psychological, to develop new skills and discover their inner spirituality. Others join communities, religious groups or renounce material possessions and become itinerant travellers or in old fashioned terms 'hippies'. Through this they discover whatever they lack in their current state (hopefully) and become a better or more effective person. Others use these discoveries to enrich themselves or manage better in their existing lives. Whatever the reason or outcome personal discovery is a huge industry and an integral part of our society.

For more information on this area you could investigate the self-help, self- improvement section of a book store or get on YouTube and type these terms in. You will get plenty of ideas and advice!

Inner Discovery

'The greatest discovery of my generation is that man can alter his life simply by altering his attitude of mind.'

JAMES ADAMS

The concept of inner discovery is closely aligned with the previous topic and can be seen similarly yet it is more aligned with exceptional circumstances. For example some people learn much about themselves during physical, emotional or psychologically stressful times and are astounded by the inner strength they have while others around them break down or fail to cope. Others find inner strength through meditation, retreats, or extremes such as becoming a hermit and focusing on the inner person. This concept of personal enlightenment is also a business in the modern world and you can get coaches who will work with you to find your inner self through various processes of discovery.

If you are looking for examples to use in your related material try googling the term and you will find a whole range of programs, coaches and books that will help you find your inner self. Dag Hammarskjold (former UN Secretary General) said 'The longest journey is the journey inwards. Of him who has chosen his destiny, who has started upon his quest for the source of his being.'

Discovery through Travel

The idea of discovery through travel is one of the first things that occur to people when they hear the word discovery. As Martin Buber(Austrian-born 20th Century Jewish philosopher) stated, 'All journeys have secret destinations of which the traveller is unaware'. This sense of travel making discoveries is well documented and became even more prominent as people began to sail widely across the seas to discover 'new' lands, many of which had been occupied by their indigenous peoples for centuries. Travel was, and to some extent still is, associated with an adventure, a journey, to test the boundaries of what we already know and seeing how far we can take the new experience and how it changes us. What we discover on our travels is revealing and often confronting.

> *"Adventure is a path. Real adventure—self-determined, self-motivated, often risky—forces you to have firsthand encounters with the world. The world the way it is, not the way you imagine it. Your body will collide with the earth and you will bear witness. In this way you will be compelled to grapple with the limitless kindness and bottomless cruelty of humankind—and perhaps realize that you yourself are capable of both. This will change you. Nothing will ever again be black-and-white."*
>
> **– MARK JENKINS**
>
> (HTTP://MATADORNETWORK.COM/BNT/50-MOST-INSPIRING-TRAVEL-QUOTES-OF-ALL-TIME/#RCM3GIDFT04P07MB.99)

Discovery through travel brings this kind of change and it may be a simpler thing such as understanding another culture, disrupting a prejudice or habit, making a friend or discovering some amazing natural beauty. Discovery through travel is one of the most written about and frequently mentioned ideas when discussing the concept. Travel has certainly changed over the centuries, even in the past decade travel to distant places has become commonplace. Air travel has especially become less than a special thing for the privileged or extremely adventurous than it was in the beginning. Think back to the times when to travel from place to place by foot or by horse was a major event. From the Middle Ages through to the later eighteenth century many people had never ventured beyond their village, apart from an infrequent trip to the nearest town. This idea leads us to consider the idea of the journey.

Discovery through Journey

This is an idea common to many areas of the discovery concept. Often the two words are associated if we think of the journey as a process not just a physical movement. Often discoveries are made on the journey rather than at the destination. The word journey has also been applied to abstract concepts. Lyndon Johnson, the American President, described peace as a deliberate process: 'Peace is a journey of a thousand miles and it must be taken one step at a time'. We have all heard the quote by Lao Tzu 'A journey of a thousand miles must begin with one step'.

The concept of journey leading to discovery is a constant in modern film and literature and it has been extensively studied in works such as Joseph Campbell's *The Hero's Journey* which organises the journey into specific stages that are common across all cultures. While each journey and even each stage of the journey allows us to discover something about ourselves or the world around us it is a very individual thing despite the cross-cultural commonalities.

As Marcel Proust (19th and 20th Century Fench novelist) stated, 'We don't receive wisdom; we must discover it for ourselves after a journey that no one can take for us or spare us.'

The physical journey could be local, in the same country, overseas or even in space, a place, many science fiction texts take us. Fantasy writers create journeys of discovery in worlds of imagination and invention. Film also focuses on the concept of discovery through journey as we see in the appalling range of road trip movies that seem so appealing to teen audiences. More serious films examine personal independence, the human condition and how one can even discover something on the journey that will change or even save humanity. You will find many examples of this in film but try and choose something where the discovery has some significant personal and/or social impact and you can discuss technique. Remember the idea of the journey as being inextricably linked to the concept of discovery as you make your way through the Area of Study.

Scientific and Technological Discovery

'Scientists have become the bearers of the torch of discovery in our quest for knowledge'

STEPHEN HAWKING

Foremost in areas of discovery in many people's thoughts are the breakthroughs made in science and technology. They have immediate and significant impact on individuals and the way they interface with the world.

Examples of the impact of technology include:

- increased internet usage has led to the rise of social networking.

- miniaturisation of hand-held devices such as the iPad have enabled people to communicate easily and more often.
- rapid changes in the way that data is stored such as the increased use of cloud-storage services has facilitated the development of much more flexible devices.

Einstein pointed out 'The process of scientific discovery is, in effect, a flight from wonder.' This is central to much of the debate that has raged over science in the past century or so. How do we progress scientifically and technologically and still maintain a moral and ethical basis? Should we chase many of the ideas that have arisen? For example the machines of war, the chemicals that kill and the genetic manipulations that can lead to social engineering. Should there be limits and controls and if so how much? Discoveries can be fraught with danger on many levels.

While it is part of discovery to imagine and test the boundaries and seek new ways, it is also probably integral to human nature. With these new technologies the consequences are even greater than in the past as more people can be affected, more invasively and quickly. Dangers emerge as people discover new methods of being destructive, such as invading computers to distort programs with viruses or stealing through cybercrimes. This is a growing and important area of research.

Humanity must also grapple with the discovery of things such as climate change and environmental issues that are the result of industrialisation through discovered technologies. The consequences of many of the discoveries in the latter half of the last century are still being felt and new discoveries are needed to solve these problems. Discovery is cyclical and never-ending.

Discovery as Creating New From Old

This is an intriguing idea probably best summed up in the idea of recycling materials to create something new. Old tyres can be used as softfall for children's playgrounds, old ideas can be given new form, new ways can be thought up to approach a topic. Even just drawing attention to a common feature can enable people to discover something about it.

One example might be the light show Vivid which featured in Sydney. Prominent buildings such as the Opera House were illuminated with an exciting coloured light show. The buildings around the harbour foreshores were visible and bathed in psychedelic colours. People flocked to see the spectacle and the show received great reviews. The reactions evoked by the light show captured the idea of discovery and re-invention as otherwise familiar images were seen in an entirely new way. The sense of wonder and amazement experienced by young children observing the show was evidence of their discovery.

Sometimes a newly discovered thing can be as simple as reading a novel previously read or re-watching a film seen years before and getting something new or different from it. Great artists always borrow from the past and rearrange it into new discoveries fortheir audience. Ideas such as this have led to new movements in the Arts or new methods of approaching a topic that casts new light on it.

Learning as Discovery

Learning in itself is a discovery that can make significant changes to an individual or a group. When we learn something that can be applied it is a small but potentially significant discovery for the individual or group. One significant piece of learning was the manipulation of fire, another the growing of crops, developing shelter and so on. While these are major discoveries other learning can be especially important for the individual. One example might be a breakthrough in reading or the ability to analyse and manipulate information to create something new. Consider this aspect of discovery as it can link to the other areas and be useful as an overriding idea to utilise as a thesis for the Area of Study essay.

Detection as Discovery

> *'The basis of drama is... The struggle of the hero toward a specific goal at the end of which he realises that what kept him from it was, in the lesser drama, civilisation and, in the greater drama, the discovery of something that he did not set out to discover but which can be seen retrospectively as inevitable.'*
>
> **DAVID MAMET**

The concept of detection as discovery is the integral aspect of the success of the eternally popular crime fiction genre and is also a major aspect of thrillers and similar literature, film and the visual arts. Paintings, for example, prove excellent material, to demonstrate how an individual can deduce something different from the same work as the person next to them. Detection, however, in its truest form is hightly valued by audiences as it is about discovering the truth through clues.

Much literature has been written in this quest to make sense of a world where justice sometimes appears to be lacking. Of course the detective genre has changed much over the years and these variations have come to suit changing audiences and contexts but this search for truth has rarely varied despite the form in which it is presented. Audiences love the sense of discovery in detection and an examination of any television or film guide will attest to the fact, as will an examination of library bookshelves.

"HOLMES GAVE ME A SKETCH OF THE EVENTS."

The Psychology of Discovery

'There'll always be serendipity involved in discovery'

JEFF BUZOS

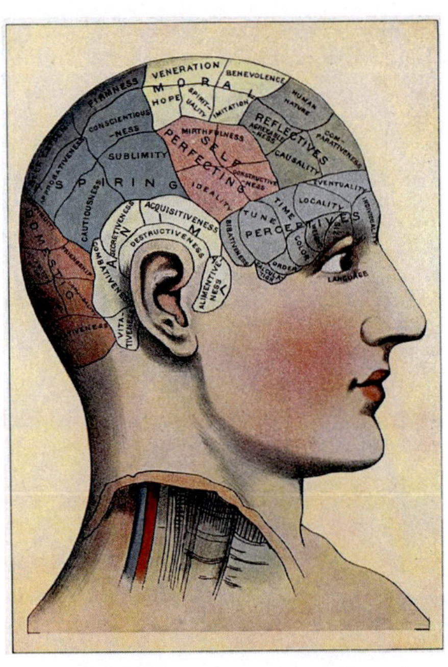

When I alluded to the innate need for discovery in the human psyche it wasn't superficial. The need for humanity to move ahead, to discover and to break boundaries is an important part of humanity's development and seems ingrained in us. The push to conquer new boundaries, to test, to push, to break boundaries is inherent in all development. Even if the discovery is the taste of a new food, the thrill of a new friend, or the discovery of any other sensory pleasure, it is a pleasure psychologically important to human development. The American writer Pearl S. Buck, who died in 1973, said that the basic discovery is the 'discovery of the relationship between men and women.' This is still true today.

There is something basic at an emotional level about discovery that attracts us to it. The new is important, broadening and thought provoking and this affects us on a psychological level. It is the emotional response that keeps people seeking the new, to discover and to absorb. This concept of the impact of discovery on our psyche is important as it is also a useful link to each of the texts and your related material. It may be a useful concept to enable you to link your ideas together. Think about the basic psychological drives that motivate us and how they are important in all our discoveries.

Nationalism, Capitalism and other 'isms' as Drivers of Discovery

'People acting in their own self-interest is the fuel for all the discovery, innovation, and prosperity that powers the world'

JOHN STOSSEL

The idea that the 'isms' are drivers of discovery may not be appealing to some but there is no doubt that many of the discoveries of the last few centuries have been driven by them. One example is the race to land on the moon or the space race. This led to some awesome discoveries yet was driven by the great Cold War divide between the Communist Russian dictatorship and the American capitalist democratic system. Buoyed by the need to be first to set foot on the moon and discover what was there, billions were spent in making this happen.

Earlier still, the drive by nations such as Spain, Portugal and England to colonise the 'New World', particularly Africa and the Americas, led to many discoveries. National pride here was mixed with the drive for resources to support their ideology: religious, capitalist. communist or nationalist. This also led to many negatives such as exploitation but much was forgiven in the race to conquer lands and spread 'civilisation'.

Capitalism, whatever your political belief, has been one of the greatest engines to drive discoveries over the centuries. This striving to produce product faster, more efficiently and thus, cheaply, has driven much innovation, prompted development of new technologies and resulted in new products. The instinct to improve and achieve is driven to its purest form by the capitalist system. It is not prudent here to discuss the pros and cons of the system itself but rather to recognise that it is a consummate motivator to *Discovery*. Gordon Gecko's quote from the film, *Wall Street*, sums up this philosophy brilliantly,

> *'Greed is right, greed works. Greed clarifies, cuts through and captures the essence of the evolutionary spirit. Greed in all of its forms; greed for life, for money, for love, knowledge has marked the upward surge of mankind.'*

Negative Aspects of Discovery

While we all have a positive image of discovery it is important to remember that it has negative aspects as well. For example, many of the early explorers who set out to discover new lands ended up dead. History is littered with such examples and many have gone down as glorious failures. One example is the story of Burke and Wills in Australia but you could also examine the exploration of the Antarctic and Arctic which have many failed expeditions. Other negatives can be found in the concept of discovering dreams of riches such as El Dorado or King Solomon's Mines.

The 'discovery' of new lands by European eadventurers led to the exploitation of discovered natural resources. Indigenous peoples, considered uneducated savages, were often enslaved. The 'slave trade' was a negative bi-product of this period of exploitation and discovery.

Away from this idea of exploration we can also have negatives in discoveries which yield promise such as nuclear power. This 'clean fuel' has been used for destructive purposes and Oppenheimer has said of his team's creation of the atomic bomb that it was a mistake. Many discoveries have been used negatively in war and in commerce for power and/or gain. We have even experienced psychological discoveries being used for brainwashing and other pernicious purposes. We have also mentioned the 'isms' that drive discovery and these can be negatively used as well. Communism killed millions and enslaved nations, patriotism in its extreme can lead to discovery but has impacted negatively on native populations and led to war.

Remember when you select a text for your related material or study a text there may be negatives to engage with that will enhance your understanding of the concept of discovery. Look for them to broaden your knowledge and ability to write clearly and formulate your own opinions.

Afterword on Discovery

'The pace of discovery is going unbelievably fast'

JAMES WATSON

Discovery is also about **possibility**, the idea that something in an imagination can be made real and attainable. Discovery is sometimes seeing the obvious and making use of it. Above all it entails faith/ dreaming and an insatiable curiosity. When you read about many discoveries they are truly tales of failure with one success. Many stories tell of years of pain, toil, ridicule, dismal progress and rejection before success is achieved. Edison made a thousand bulbs before he got one to work. Failure is a constant with many people you will study in this topic until they discover their dream. They maintained their faith in the face of great adversity and this is what makes them discoverers. If it were easy everyone would do it!

Discoverers are also people who see what others have missed. Often they simply look at something in a new way. To look for new ideas, we must maintain an open mind. To discover for ourselves the mysteries of texts and how to unlock them, we must develop strategies for analysis and perseverence to achieve understanding.

Perhaps you think everything has been discovered as a pessimist might, but discoverers are optimists, people who continually seek success, or insight in achieving their goals or realising their dreams.

Questions for Discovery

- Define the term 'discovery' in your own words.
- How can discovery and possibility be connected?
- Discuss what the term discovery means to you.
- Create your own list of synonyms and antonyms for the word discovery. Then choose two or three to use in your writing so the word discovery won't be repeated.
- Science is often connected with discovery. Research one such instance and write two paragraphs on it connecting it thematically to your set text.
- What is positive about discovery?
- Discuss the idea that discovery can be a two-edged sword.
- Discuss one discovery and the benefits of that discovery to humanity.
- Do you think the concept of discovery is integral to detective fiction? Explain your answer fully.
- Analyse one 'ism' and how discovery has been driven by it.
- Discuss some of the negatives associated with the concept of discovery?

STUDYING A FICTION TEXT

The medium of any text is very important. If a text is a novel this must not be forgotten. Novels are *read*. This means you should refer to the "reader" but the "responder" can also be used when you are referring to the audience of the text.

The marker will want to know you are aware of the text as a novel and that you have considered its effect as a written text.

Remembering a fiction text is a written text also means when you are exploring *how* the composer represents his/her ideas you MUST discuss language techniques. This applies to any response you do using a novel, irrespective of the form the response is required to be in.

Language techniques are all the devices the author uses to represent his or her ideas. They are the elements of a fiction that are manipulated by authors to make any novel represent its ideas effectively! You might also see them referred to as stylistic devices or narrative techniques.

Every fiction uses language techniques differently. Some authors have their own favourite techniques that they are known for. Others use a variety to make their text achieve its purpose.

Some common language techniques are shown on the diagram that follows.

LANGUAGE TECHNIQUES

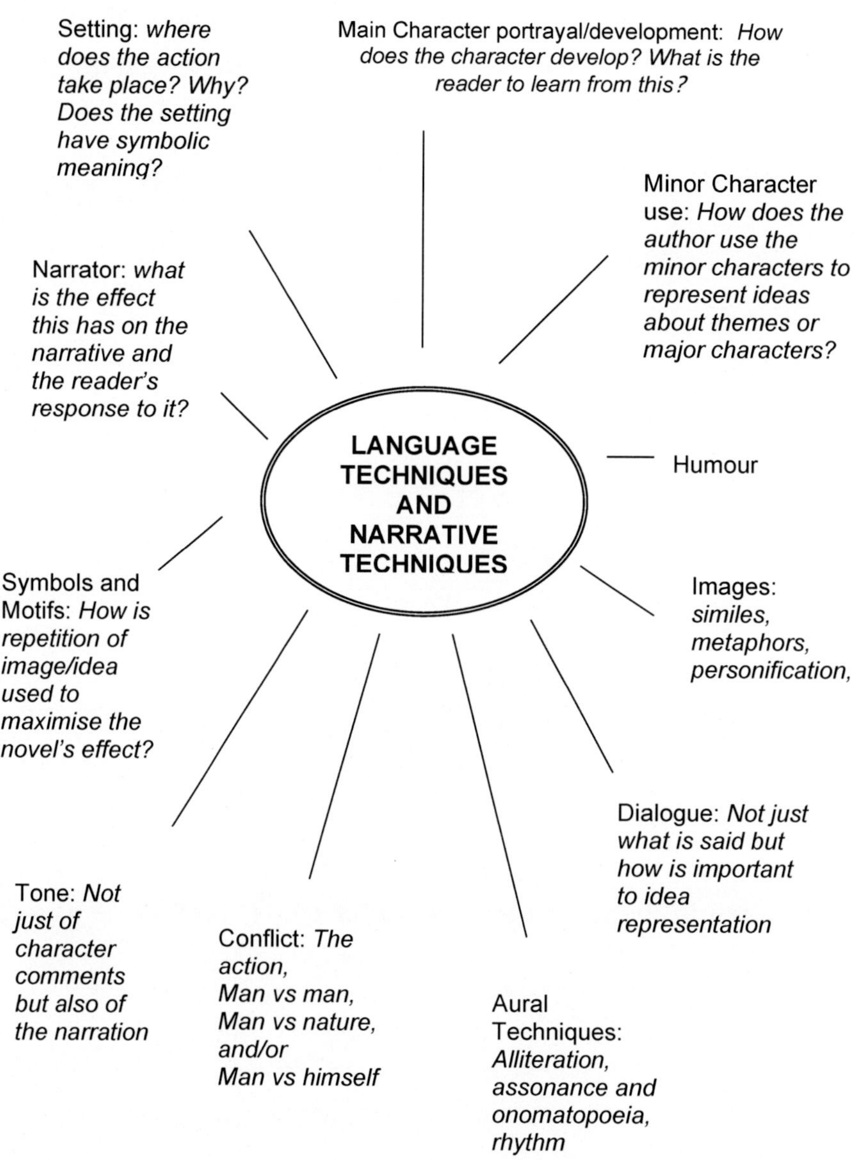

THE AUTHOR

The following extract is an extended and detailed adaptation from

HTTP://EN.WIKIPEDIA.ORG/WIKI/KATE_CHOPIN

and it gives a brief overview of her life. More detailed biographical information can be found at:

HTTP://WWW.KATECHOPIN.ORG/BIOGRAPHY.SHTML

HTTP://WWW.VCU.EDU/ENGWEB/WEBTEXTS/HOUR/KATEBIO.HTML

HTTP://AMERICANLITERATURE.COM/AUTHOR/KATE-CHOPIN/BIO-BOOKS-STORIES

HTTP://EMPIREZINE.COM/SPOTLIGHT/CHOPIN/CHOPIN1.HTM

Kate Chopin, born **Katherine O'Flaherty** (February 8, 1850 — August 22, 1904), was an American author of short stories and novels. The Southern feel to her works begins in her Missouri childhood where she was educated well and became a member of the St Louis social scene. She married Oscar Chopin a member of a well-recognized Louisiana Creole family. Like her character Edna, Chopin also sought to escape domestic life which earned her some negative gossip.

From 1892 to 1895, she wrote short stories for both children and adults which were published in such magazines as *Atlantic Monthly, Vogue, The Century Magazine,* and *The Youth's Companion.* Her major works were two short story collections, *Bayou Folk* (1894) and *A Night in Acadie* (1897). Her important short stories included "Desiree's Baby," a tale of miscegenation in antebellum Louisiana (published in 1893), "The Story of an Hour" (1894), and "The Storm"(1898). "The Storm" is a sequel to "The 'Cadian Ball," which appeared in her first collection of short stories, *Bayou Folk.* Chopin also wrote two novels: *At Fault* (1890) and *The Awakening* (1899), which are set in New Orleans and Grand Isle, respectively. The people in her stories are usually inhabitants of Louisiana. Many of her works are set in Natchitoches in north central Louisiana. It is said that by focusing on a particular setting she could not only capture individual idiosyncrasies and passions so that readers thought they were not widespread in society.

The Awakening was her final work and it was extremely controversial and not widely accepted because of the content, mainly the sexuality displayed by Edna. Certainly the attitudes in it toward women and motherhood were not accepted, even in her home state where women were still, by law, the property of their husband. Decades after her death, Chopin was widely recognized as one of the leading writers of her time. In 1915, Fred Lewis Pattee wrote, "some of [Chopin's] work is equal to the best that has been produced in France or even in America. [She displayed] what may be described as a native aptitude for narration amounting almost to genius." She is now considered by some to have been a forerunner of the feminist authors of the 20th century because of her views and writing style.

CONTEXT

The context of *The Awakening* is of particular importance in our understanding of the text and the discoveries that Edna makes on her way to her finding freedom and passion. You will read much about this on your way through this study guide but here I will try to give you a concise overview of the period. Firstly you need to read the setting section where there is a detailed analysis of the settings of Louisiana and New Orleans to get a feel of the novel and where Chopin herself lived. The graphic below also gives an indication of the Creole housing and attire of the period.

The reception of *The Awakening* gives us a sound indication of the context of the period and at

HTTP://WWW.LITERATURE-STUDY-ONLINE.COM/ESSAYS/CHOPIN.HTML

Jones writes,

> '*The Awakening* was published in 1899, and it immediately created a controversy. Contemporaries of Kate Chopin (1851–1904) were shocked by her depiction of a woman with active sexual desires, who dares to leave her husband and have an affair. Instead of condemning her protagonist, Chopin maintains a neutral, non-judgmental tone throughout and appears to even condone her character's unconventional actions. Kate Chopin was socially ostracised after the publication of her novel, which was almost forgotten until the second half of the twentieth century. *The Awakening* has been reclaimed by late twentieth-century theorists who see Edna Pontellier as the prototypical feminist. ...Society of the nineteenth-century gave a heightened meaning to what it means to be a woman. According to the commonly known 'code of true womanhood', women were supposed to be docile, domestic creatures, whose main concerns in life were to be the raising of their children and submissiveness to their husbands.'

In her context Chopin was ostracised for her views but more modern audiences critically applaud her for her forthright views which have become more acceptable. One example is,

Barbara C. Ewell, "*The Awakening* in a Course on Women in Literature"

***Approaches to Teaching Chopin's The Awakening,* ed. Koloski (New York: MLA, 1988)**

> '... the novel offers a paradigmatic tale of a woman's abortive struggle toward selfhood in an oppressive, uncomprehending society....

The pertinence of Edna's dilemma—how to be an individual in a society that insists she play specific roles—is certainly a key to its fascination since it uniquely engages both younger students (who are much involved in articulating their selves) and older students (who are well aware of the compromising forces of social reality). But in presenting the terms of that dilemma, Chopin exposes a number of specifically female concerns, issues that are inevitably the focus of women's studies: the nature of female sexuality, the conventional opposition of romance and passion, the moral isolation of women in patriarchal systems, the role of female friendship, the importance of the body and the physical world to self-realization, the ambivalence toward children and childbearing.'

HTTP://PEOPLE.VIRGINIA.EDU/~SFR/ENLT255/AWAKENINGNOW.HTML

It is important for you to remember that the discoveries that Edna makes throughout the novel are ones that were not acceptable in her time and certainly even beyond the comprehension of her husband. It is with this in mind that we begin our reading.

PLOT OUTLINE

It is summer holiday time for the Pontellier family

Holidays are taken on the Lebrun island

Here we are introduced to all the main characters such as the Lebrun's, Ratignolles and Mademoiselle Reisz.

Edna Pontellier, the protagonist, begins to fall in love with Robert Lebrun.

Edna begins to find herself and distance herself.

Back in New Orleans her behavior changes and she is less domestic.

She begins to visit Mademoiselle Reisz to learn about Robert who has escaped to Mexico

Edna becomes estranged from her husband, Leonce, who goes to Doctor Mandalet for help with a situation he doesn't comprehend.

While Mr Pontellier is away on business and the children are at the grandparents she holds a farewell dinner at the house.

Edna moves out to the 'pigeon-house' to begin a new life.

She has some money from her racing wins and begins to see Alcee Arobin there.

Edna completely breaks from her old life as best she can

Her art becomes her work

Edna is becoming more aware of herself

Arobin and Edna begin an affair of sorts

Robert comes back from Mexico.

They avoid each other but want to be together.

Robert and Edna declare their love

Edna leaves him to attend Madame Ratignolle's birth.

After the birth she is reminded by Madame not to forget the children.

On the way home she confesses some of her issues to the Doctor.

When she returns Robert is gone. All she has is a note professing his love and his good-bye.

Edna heads out to the island having thought through her issues.

Edna swims out thinking of her life and becomes exhausted.

PLOT SUMMARY

The Awakening

I

Here we are introduced to Mr Pontellier and the Lebrun cottages where the families come to spend time. He is described closely and we are given insights into some of the other inhabitants of the summer retreat. We see the first interaction between himself and his wife, Edna who is the protagonist of *The Awakening*. Here they seem comfortable and set into a married routine of knowing each other as evidenced by the final dinner conversation and familial piety.

II

Edna Pontellier is described so we now begin to know her intimately and we are invited into the world of the relationship she shares with Robert Lebrun and how he fits into the scene. Mrs Pontellier is an American woman from Mississippi who only has 'a small infusion of French which seemed to have been lost in dilution.' (p47)

III

Later that night Mr Pontellier returns after missing dinner and he wakes her. He is upset that she 'evinced so little interest in things which concerned him, and valued so little his conversation.' He looks in on the children and thinks one has a fever which she knows is untrue but he chastises her in a 'monotonous, insistent way' and goes to the child. He goes to sleep and she heads outside to sit on the porch chair and begins to cry. An 'indescribable oppression' overcomes her but the mosquitoes drive her inside.

The next morning he gives her half the money he won at billiards and he seems more composed than he was the night before, promising to buy her sister a great wedding present as he heads back to the city for work. Later in the week he sends her a box of goodies from New Orleans which she shares with the others families. They declare her husband the best 'in the world' and she has to agree.

IV

Mrs Pontellier is not a maternal woman and this is what her husband has noticed. On holiday at Grand Isle the other women certainly were and Mrs Ratignolle was the perfection of this. She is described in great detail and her charms are obvious. She and Mrs Pontellier are good friends and they spend time together despite Mrs Ratignolle having a 'condition' having had three babies in seven years and planning another. Mrs Pontellier was not 'thoroughly at home in the society of Creoles' despite having married one and she thinks they have no 'prudery' and she is shocked at some of the things they say and read.

V

Robert lives in Mrs Pontellier's shadow for a month and does this each year with one of the guests. She does not know at times what to make of him but he has never expressed 'words of love' to her as he had to her friend. Mrs Pontellier paints a little to fill time and her portrait of Madame Ratignolle is not like her but 'satisfying' nonetheless. Edna watches Madame Ratignolle with her children and then heads to the beach for a bath with Robert.

VI

Edna realises she has 'contradictory impulses' and she is becoming more aware and thoughtful about her situation as an 'individual'. This is unsettling to her. In this section there is also a foreshadowing of events that come later in:

> *'The touch of the sea speaks to the soul. The touch of the sea is sensuous, enfolding the body in its soft, close embrace.'*

In many ways this short section is a synopsis of events in the novel and the changes in Edna Pontellier over the time period of the novel.

VII

Edna loosens up a little that summer on Grand Isle from the more reticent woman that she had always been. One cause was Adele Ratignolle who was a 'sensuous' woman who was a good friend. They head down to the beach after we are given a detailed description of her by Chopin. Edna focuses on the sea and her thoughts drift until Adele draws her back into a conversation about life and religion. Adele strokes Edna's hand in a 'gentle caress' and it is initially confusing as she has never experienced anything like this, especially from her sister and friends. We read of some of her past attachments and infatuations while learning that her marriage to Leonce Pontellier was 'purely an accident' and she would have married another had he returned her love. She had been mistaken to think she and Leonce could have passion and she became fond of him. She even was 'fond' of her children but when they were away she was 'free'.

Edna confides some of this to Mrs Ratignolle during the summer yet the comfort of this day is interrupted by Robert and the children who arrive and Mrs Pontellier joins them. Mrs Ratignolle asks Robert to accompany her back to the house, establishing the scenario for the following section.

VIII

Mrs Ratignolle asks Robert to 'let Mrs Pontellier alone' as she is worried that the lady will take his actions and words seriously. The subject changes as she relates some gossip about Alcée Arobin and another affair. When they arrive at her cottage he tells her Mrs Pontellier could never take him seriously and then makes her some bouillon as she is tired. A pair of lovers who are also there for the summer appear and Chopin has them as ephemeral extras throughout, living in a world apart.

Robert goes to his mother and talks to her while she uses the big sewing-machine in a 'desultory' way. She comes to life when Victor is seen from the window. He is Robert's younger brother and a man 'with a temper that invited violence and a will which no ax could break'. Robert has hopes of achieving something with his career in Mexico and she has a letter that may help his advancement but the conversation turns back to Mrs Pontellier.

IX

A few weeks have passed and a special concert is being performed on a Saturday night. The children perform and, when they are finished, the adults also dance to music played by Madame Ratignolle. After the success of the ice-cream, the children are sent to bed and Mademoiselle Reisz comes to play the piano. She is described as a 'homely woman' who has 'no taste in dress'. Yet she plays beautifully and Edna, who is 'fond of music' as it evokes pictures in her mind, is nearly overcome with passion.

Mademoiselle Reisz notices this and tells Edna that she is the only one worth playing for. Robert then proposes a bath, 'at that mystic hour and under that mystic moon.'

X

Everyone agrees to go and Robert walks behind the lovers as they want to 'hold themselves apart'. As Edna walks with her husband she thinks of Robert as she misses his attentions when he is away from her. The sea is quiet and she has been learning to swim all summer. That night she swims out further than ever before, 'daring and reckless', and her teachers all praise her ability. She swims out to lose herself and nearly succeeds having a 'quick vision of death' but gets back to shore. This foreshadowing reinforces the earlier idea of the sea and water that recurs throughout. She tells Leonce that she thought she might die and he assures her he was keeping a close eye on her.

She goes to the bath house, dries herself and begins to walk back, ignoring all the others who swam. Mrs Lebrun calls her 'capricious' and Leonce agrees that 'sometimes' she is. Robert follows her and she admits she was 'stirred' by Mademoiselle Reisz's music. Robert creates a tale of a Gulf spirit that has chosen her but she rebukes him for flippancy. Taking his arm they get to the hammock where she rests. He stays with her until the others return and she watches him walk away.

XI

Edna's husband finds her awake on the hammock and wonders what she is doing. He wants her in bed but she refuses to his annoyance. Normally she would have just done what he wanted but this night her 'will had blazed up' and she refuses. He remains awake, drinking a bottle of wine and smoking cigars. Eventually she rises and goes to bed but Leonce stays up smoking.

XII

Mrs Pontellier doesn't sleep well and gets up early to follow her impulses. Most of the others are still asleep but the lovers are up and she sends the 'little negro girl' to get Robert as she plans to go to church. Of course he responds and his face has a 'quiet glow' when they meet. Neither thinks anything unusual in the situation. They have coffee and a roll before getting into the boat. Edna looks at Mariequita and the girl talks to Robert about Edna in the local dialect which Edna does not understand. As they sail across the bay Robert gives Edna his full attention and he asks her to visit Grande Terre with him. They plan an outing and as they head to the 'quaint little Gothic church' Mariequita gives Robert a 'look of childish ill-humor and reproach'.

XIII

Edna leaves the stifling church as she needs fresh air and Robert follows her. He takes her to Madame Antoine's place where she is shown a room with a great four-poster bed upon which she could 'repose'. Edna loosens her clothing and luxuriates in the bed until she falls asleep. When she awakens the mosquito net has been drawn over her and she feels as if she slept for a long time. She peers through the curtains, sees Robert and wonders where the others from the boat party are. Edna completes her toilet and then eats, finally going out to Robert where they joke about how long she has slept. He tells her the others have gone hours ago and Robert assures her that Leonce will not be worried as she is with him. Madame Antoine returns full of stories and they listen until nightfall when they return in Tonie's boat.

XIV

On returning Madame Ratignolle attends to the children telling her Etienne, the youngest, had been naughty. Edna is also informed Leonce had been initially concerned but upon being reassured had gone to Klein's to meet another man about business. Then Madame returns to her husband and Robert helps Edna place her child into bed. She reminds him they have been together for a whole day before he leaves. She thinks about what had been different about that summer as she waits for her husband to return. As she sits Robert's song haunts 'her memory'.

XV

Edna gets the news one evening at dinner that Robert is heading to Mexico and leaving that very evening. She had been with him that same day and he had said nothing so her look is of 'bewilderment'. She asks the group how he can leave so quickly ignoring the fact he is there. He begins to defend himself but Mrs Lebrun calls for order at the table and after some interjections by Victor, Robert explains himself. He is going to meet a man at Vera Cruz and to make the appointment has to leave now. The only people who were not listening were the lovers who are still off in their own world and grateful of the disruption.

Everyone begins to comment on Mexicans in general and Mrs Ratignolle considers them a treacherous people, unscrupulous and revengeful, despite only ever knowing one. Victor also joins in. Finally Edna gets to ask Robert what time he leaves. He replies ten. She immediately leaves for her own room where she tends to things and puts the children to bed. Despite being invited back over to the house to see Robert depart she chooses to stay. Robert comes to her and says he doesn't want to depart from her in ill-humour and she admits she will miss him.

He promises to write and then walks away into the darkness. Her eyes are brimming with tears and she realises the 'symptoms of infatuation'. She comprehends the significance of what she has lost i.e. what 'her impassioned, newly awakened being demanded.'

XVI

Mademoiselle Reisz asks Edna if she misses Robert. It is a question that has been echoing in Edna's mind. Indeed Robert's absence had changed things and Edna had begun to spend time with Mrs Lebrun where she looked at old photos of Robert as a child. Unfortunately there were no recent pictures to fill the 'void and wilderness' he had left behind. Robert has sent a letter to his mother and it was of extreme interest to Edna. It was only brief but it did mention Mrs Pontellier yet Edna is jealous as he wrote to his mother and not her.

Everyone knows and accepts she would miss him, even her husband. He admits he had seen Robert in the city where they talked about the young man's prospects in Mexico. Edna does not think it strange talking of Robert to her husband as she had always kept her 'thoughts and emotions' to herself. Edna and Madame Ratignolle had once argued when Edna proclaimed she would never sacrifice herself for her children or anyone. The Madame cannot comprehend this.

Edna tells Mademoiselle Reisz that she does miss Robert and then she asks her to bathe, an idea the older woman rejects out of hand. Edna mollifies her with chocolates and then Mademoiselle tells her that Victor is Mrs Lebrun's favourite son, not Robert, yet Victor is the sort of man that needs a thrashing occasionally to keep him in line. Edna goes in to swim while the Mademoiselle waited and they walk back together in an amiable manner. Edna obtains the Mademoiselle's address and they arrange a visit.

XVII

In New Orleans the Pontellier's own a home on Esplanade Street of which Mr Pontellier is particularly proud, especially of his possessions. Tuesday was Mrs Pontellier's reception day with a stream of visitors that had come traditionally for the six years of her marriage. Mr Pontellier also had a routine and they had a routine together until one Tuesday when Edna goes out and one isn't home when the visitors call. Mr Pontellier is much put out and he wants to know why, disbelieving her when she tells him she left no excuse. She asks for the visitors' cards and while they are gathered by the servant he complains about the soup. The dinner goes badly from that point and he leaves to dine at the club. She continues her dinner alone. On previous occasions such scenes had upset her but that evening 'her eyes flamed with some inward fire that lighted them.' She leaves the room and walks about, even throwing off her wedding ring and stomping on it. She then, in a passion, seizes a vase and destroys it on the hearth. The maid comes in to clean up and returns Edna's ring, which she puts back on her finger.

XVIII

The next day Mr Pontellier asks Edna to look at new fixtures with him for the house. She declines and he thinks her ill yet all she feels is bored with everything around her. She can't even chastise the cook because Leonce had done that, and in a way she never could. Edna begins to look at her old sketches, finds a few she likes and gathers them up to take to Madame Ratignolle's with her. They had maintained their acquaintance from the summer and we learn the Ratignolles are well respected and have wonderful soirees, musical evenings, which are extremely popular.

Madame Ratignolle is engaged in domestic duties but hands them to her servant. Mrs Pontellier asks her friend to evaluate the sketches. Madame Ratignolle loves the works and Edna gives her some just before Mr Ratignolle comes home for midday dinner. He thinks Edna needs a tonic but it is their domestic harmony that has depressed her. She sees nothing there for her and knows that life is not for her as it lacks 'life's delirium'.

XIX

Edna evaluates her behaviour after dinner but she does abandon Tuesday visitations and does things according to her fancy. Mr Pontellier is completely 'bewildered' by her change and cannot understand why she will not complete her domestic duties. When they argue she tells him she wants to paint and he says she can paint but still do her tasks but she refuses to engage and says 'you bother me' to him. He thinks she is growing 'a little unbalanced mentally' yet she is just 'becoming herself'. This can be seen as a process of self discovery.

Edna begins to paint, first the children, then the staff and this brings back memories of the summer. She begins to be happy, especially when alone. However, some days she was unhappy and could not work.

XX

One day when in a dark mood Edna has a desire to see Mademoiselle Reisz but has lost her details and has to make a concerted effort to find her. She tracks the lady as the difficulty of the task has made her desire all the greater. She can get no help from the Ratignolles who are distanced from the lady so she goes to Mrs Lebrun where Victor opens the gate. He is pleased to see her. It is such a nice afternoon Edna sits on the porch rather than enter the house. Victor explains to her that he has just returned from the island where he lives all year, keeping it ready for the summer. He begins to reminisce about his adventures in the city when his mother arrives and interrupts. She informs Mrs Pontellier that Robert has written 'but two letters' that held very little information which Victor remembers. Robert had met his mentor, Montel, and they were doing business but with no greater financial benefit than he had in New Orleans. Edna is unhappy again as she gets no mention but Mrs Lebrun does inform her that she knows the whereabouts of Mademoiselle Reisz. Mrs Lebrun comments to Victor that Mrs Pontellier 'doesn't seem like the same woman.'

XXI

Mademoiselle Reisz had an upstairs room that had a view but was dominated by a piano. The lady was pleased to see Edna and makes coffee. They talk candidly before Mademoiselle Reisz says Robert has written to her but she refuses to let Edna see the letter. Edna tells her she is becoming an artist and begs to see the letters and hear Mademoiselle play the piano. The woman relents and Edna reads the letter while she plays. The music and the letter move her to sobbing as the shadows fill the room. The music ends and Edna leaves but not before asking to visit again.

XXII

Mr Pontellier goes to visit his old friend Dr Mandalet. He tells the Doctor that he is worried about his wife but the Doctor has seen her in the street and thinks she is a 'picture of health'. Leonce explains to him that she is behaving oddly and that her actions are hard to explain. He admits candidly that,

'Her whole attitude - toward me and everybody and everything - has changed.'

He tells that she is driving him to quarrel and the Doctor is concerned she may have been associating with 'pseudo-intellectual women'. Pontellier discloses she hasn't been associating with anyone. He reveals that she is refusing to go to her sister's wedding. After listening carefully the Doctor suggests he just leave his wife alone as they are both not qualified for these types of peculiarities in a woman. She will need an 'inspired psychologist' to deal with them. The Doctor says he will come around for dinner to see her but thinks it will pass in one or two or three months or 'possibly longer'. When Mr Pontellier has left the Doctor thinks of the question he wanted to ask in the conversation about the possibility of another man.

XXIII

Edna's father was in the city to buy a wedding present for his daughter, Janet. While Edna was not close to him he opened up a new aspect of society to her. She sketches him and they attend a soirée at the Ratignolles where Madame Ratignolle charms him, something Edna does not understand as she has no ability for coquetry. Mr Pontellier did not attend these soirees as he preferred the club. Madame Ratignolle thinks Mr Pontellier should be home more and not at the club but Edna is horrified at the thought as they have nothing to say to each other.

When the Doctor dined with them he could not find any problem with Edna and she is indeed 'radiant'. She had been to the racetrack with her father where they had met some very interesting people and even won some money. Mr Pontellier was critical of racing and this causes a dispute with his father-in-law whose side was taken by Edna. The Doctor notices she has changed and had the force of life. The company exchange stories and Edna's invented story of the lovers is well told. As the Doctor walks home he regrets going as he knows it is another man in her life and he desperately hopes it isn't Alcée Arobin.

XXIV

Edna argues strongly with her father about not attending the wedding and Mr Pontellier follows the advice he received and does not interfere with her choice. Finally he leaves and she is glad to be rid of him. Mr Pontellier follows on soon after as he intends to go to the wedding and then move on to New York for his business interests. Edna was not as sure about Leonce's leaving as she thinks of the considerations he has given her. She acts as Madame Ratignolle would have done but she is soon not unhappy about being alone as the children have gone to his parents. She has the house to herself and luxuriates in it, dining alone and even becoming a little sentimental about her family. Edna reads and then goes to bed, feeling a 'sense of restlessness...such as she had not known before'.

XXV

Edna worked on her art best on sunny days so when the weather is inclement she visits friends. She again goes to the races with Alcée Arobin and Mrs Highcamp, an unaffected blonde woman. Arobin was a man about town with, at times, an insolent manner and he admires Edna. She was very knowledgeable about horses due to her Kentucky upbringing and people even look to her to give them a 'tip'. They dined with Mrs Highcamp and then Edna is escorted home by Arobin. Arobin leaves after she agrees to go to the races with him again. Still energetic and hungry, Edna makes some supper. She wanted something to happen but she has to go to bed agitated.

Days later Arobin comes to pick her up for the races but Mrs Highcamp cannot attend and Edna cannot think of one of her acquaintances who would wish to attend so the pair go alone. Over the afternoon they become 'intimate' as he is an easy confident man and he stays to dine with her. She says she won't go to the races again as she must paint when the weather is good. He asks to see her art but she refuses and says she is excited by the afternoon's events and he must go. She feels his kiss on the back of her hand and thinks she may have betrayed not her husband, but Robert in her feelings of passion.

XXVI

Arobin sends her an apology but she feels embarrassed as it is no great matter to get a hand kissed. She sends him a note that he may call to look at her art whenever he could manage it. He comes at once and from then he comes every day until they become accustomed to each other. Once his conversation may have been embarrassing to her but now it appealed to the 'animalism that stirred impatiently within her.'

Edna often softened her 'turmoil' by visiting Mademoiselle Reisz whose presence seemed to set her spirit free. It is a miserable day and Edna is wet so she takes some brandy before revealing she intends to move out of the house and into a little house around the corner. Mademoiselle knows the reason is because the other house and its contents are Mr Pontellier's and she needs her independence. She has some means of her own and her art is beginning to sell. Edna reveals she has not told her husband and she thinks about how she will tell him and reach an understanding. Edna decides to give one final dinner at the old house before departing where they can 'laugh and be merry for once.'

Mademoiselle Reisz gives Edna another letter from Robert when she arrives and reveals Robert does not know Edna sees them as he would be angry. She states he does not write to Edna because he is in love with her and is trying to forget her. The letter reveals Robert is returning 'very soon'. They talk of love and Edna admits for the first time that she loves Robert. She is extremely pleased that he is returning and cannot hide it. On the way home she stops and buys confectionary to send to her children. At home she writes to her husband telling him of her intentions to quit the house and hold a final dinner.

XXVII

Arobin notices that she is in a good mood later that evening. She talks about defining herself and he says not to bother thinking about it. She tells him how Mademoiselle Reisz tells her things that make her think. She cites the example of the woman asking her if her wings were strong. Arobin has heard the woman is disagreeable and wants to talk about Edna. He leans forward and kisses her. She responds by holding his lips to hers. This is the 'flaming torch that kindled desire.'

XXVIII

Edna cries that night after he is gone because of the emotions that swirl in her. She feels reproach from her husband, from

Robert yet there was also understanding. She feels no shame or remorse but some regret as it was not a kiss of love.

XXIX

Edna moves on with her planned move and doesn't wait for a response from Mr Pontellier. She secures the new residence, moves all her possessions not acquired by her husband and when Arobin comes to visit finds her with her sleeves rolled up like a servant. He helps her with the work which amuses her and they talk of the dinner at the old house which she is calling a coup d'état. She says he can see her at the dinner and not before.

XXX

The dinner is not a grand one but relatively small. Only ten people come which makes it a cosy number. The guests include Mr and Mrs Merriman, Mrs Highcamp, Alcée Arobin, Mademoiselle Reisz, Victor Lebrun, Mr Gouvernail, Miss Mayblunt and Monsieur Ratignolle. The room has been redesigned and Edna is wearing her new 'cluster of diamonds' which Mr Pontellier has sent her for her birthday from New York. The dinner begins agreeably with a toast with a cocktail devised by her father and this festive mood continues. The conversation swings about between guests and each tells stories to those seated near them.

Edna's seat at the table and her posture suggest a 'regal woman… one who stands alone.' Still she is overcome with a feeling of hopelessness and a 'sense of the unattainable.' The dinner continues well. Monsieur Ratignolle is the first to leave to attend to his wife. Mademoiselle Reisz leaves with him and the party continues. Mrs Highcamp drapes Victor in a garland of roses and a scarf. He sings a song which displeases Edna and the party breaks up although Victor promises to visit Miss Highcamp at the initiation of her mother. Only Arobin is left with Edna.

XXXI

Edna tells Arobin the servants have been sent away and the house is to be locked up. They leave and she wants to take nothing more. They head to the 'pigeon-house' as the new dwelling is called because the inside is 'habitable and homelike'. He strokes her hair as they part but he continues to caress her and eventually 'she had become supple to his gentle, seductive entreaties.'

XXXII

Mr Pontellier is disapproving of her move and acts to rescue his business reputation by ordering alterations to the house and announcing a planned summer sojourn abroad while the builders were active. Edna is happy with this ruse and does nothing to disprove it. She is pleased with her own residence as it is hers. She even goes up to Iberville to spend time with her children which she seems to enjoy. She wanders the farm with them and they ask about the changes to their home. Mr Pontellier's mother, the old Madame, was glad the house was being refurbished as it gave her an excuse to keep the children. She misses them when she leaves until she gets back to the city where she is again alone.

XXXIII

Mademoiselle Reisz is occasionally absent when Edna visits, so there is a hidden key for Edna to use for entry. On this day, Mademoiselle Reisz is absent. Edna takes time to reflect. She reflects on her art, a visit from Madame Ratignolle and her warning that Edna is like a child acting without reflection at times. She suggests Edna get someone to live with her to stop the gossip and warns her against Arobin given his reputation. Later in the day, Mrs Merriman and Mrs Highcamp also visited her.

Edna sits and waits at Mademoiselle Reisz's house, looking out over the river and picking at the piano. A knock at the door announces the arrival of Robert Lebrun who makes Edna 'ill at ease'. She wonders why he hasn't come to her and he tells her he has been busy, getting his old job back and settling in. The Mexican episode had not worked out for him and as he talks she looks at him intently, noticing not much has changed. He knows her news and she enquires why he didn't write. They leave together for her home but pass her old one which he enquires about.

At the 'pigeon-house', she convinces him to stay for dinner. He finds a sketch of Arobin and asks about it before they catch up on times past which both have been thinking about. Robert thinks her 'cruel' as they sit in silence waiting for dinner to be announced.

XXXIV

The dining-room is small and as they continue on with the small talk. Even Celestine the servant joins in as she knew Robert as a child. He leaves to purchase a cigar and offers to leave but Edna says she will never tire of him. They talk of Mexican girls when Arobin arrives to say the card party at Mrs Merriman's had been cancelled. Robert leaves and Arobin says he is a fine fellow. She wants Arobin to go and he does after complimenting her. She has a 'dreamy, absent look' as he leaves. She stays in a 'stupor' thinking of Robert, being jealous of the Mexican girl and wondering if he will come back.

XXXV

The first sentence sums up Edna's mood: 'The morning was full of sunlight and hope.' She cannot forget that Mademoiselle Reisz had said Robert loved her. She gets a letter from Raoul sending her his love and telling of life at the farm. She also gets a letter from Mr Pontellier stating they can afford the overseas trip as his business was profitable and he would be back in March. Another letter came from Arobin, sending his devotion.

She replies to her children cheerfully and to her husband with friendly evasiveness as she now has no 'sense of reality' in her life which was abandoned to 'Fate'. She doesn't reply to Arobin, then paints for several hours. She is disappointed Robert does not come that day or the next or the next. She tries to avoid being where he might be despite an urge to seek him out. Arobin takes her out for a ride and they are quite discreet, dining at her place. He leaves late and for Arobin she has become more than a 'passing whim' as he had detected her 'sensuality'.

XXXVI

Edna has taken to stopping on her walks at an overlooked garden where she can have a quiet dinner. She is there when Robert enters and he says they only met by accident. It is a place he knows well too and she says they can share dinner. Edna asks why he hasn't seen her and he makes a list of excuses for her to choose from. They exchange commentary and find they share similarities in taste. Robert admits he is getting 'reckless'. They leave for her home and he stays waiting for her to wash up.

She returns to him in the shadows and bends to kiss him. They kiss and embrace with 'love and tenderness'. He admits he has been fighting his feelings for her because she was married and that he thought only of her while in Mexico. She says she is a free woman and can choose to give herself. She is not her husband's chattel. They are interrupted by a servant who says Madame Ratignolle is sick and asking for her. As they part she tells him she loves him and that he had freed her. He wants her to stay and feels he needs to 'hold her and keep her.'

XXXVII

On the way Edna meets Mr Ratignolle at the drug store and he tells her his wife will be pleased to see her. She is met by Madame complaining of the Doctor but the nurse is used to it and so is the Doctor when he comes. Madame wants Edna to stay with her at all times and this brings back memories of her own childbirth. She wishes she hadn't come and then witnesses the 'scene of torture.' At the end Adèle reminds her to 'think of the children! Remember them!'

XXXVIII

Edna is still stunned when she goes outside and refuses to ride with Doctor Mandalet. He walks with her and he says that Edna need not have been there. She admits when asked that she will not go overseas with Leonce and she wants to be left alone, except perhaps for the children. He tells her 'Nature takes no account of moral consequences' and that he feels that she is in trouble. He offers to help her and she thanks him but asks him not to blame her. He says he will if she doesn't come to see him but she is not to blame herself.

At home she sits on the porch and goes back to when she was with Robert, feeling his touch. She hears Adèle's words about the children and thinks she will remember them tomorrow. She goes in but Robert is gone, leaving her a note which reads,

'I love you. Good-by - because I love you.'

She sits up all night on the sofa not uttering a word.

XXXIX

Victor is working on the summer house at the island and teasing Mariequita about Mrs Pontellier's dinner when suddenly the lady herself appears, looking a 'little travel-stained'.

She shocks them both at her appearance and they make some hasty arrangements for her stay. She tells them she intends to swim before dinner and they can't dissuade her. She heads down to the water thinking of her life but the children still hang over her. She just wanted Robert but she realised he too, one day, would go. The children are her 'soul's slavery' yet she knew 'a way to elude them'.

Edna puts on her bathing suit that is still hanging in the bath-house but on the beach casts the clothes off her and goes naked 'like some new-born creature' while walking into the water. She begins to swim out into the sea and it enfolds her. She thinks of her life as she swims: her childhood, Leonce and her children, Robert's note and finally she thinks the Doctor may have understood but it is too late. She has swum too far and is exhausted. Her final thoughts are of her childhood.

Questions for Plot

1. Discuss in a paragraph or two Edna Pontellier's life at the beginning of the novel.

2. Analyse one incident on the island such as the trip to the church or Robert's leaving for Mexico in terms of how we see Edna.

3. What changes her perception of life? Is it an incident on the summer island or something back in New Orleans?

4. Discuss in detail two of the changes she makes to her life.

5. Analyse these changes in terms of how they affect ONE other character in the novel.

6. How do you see Edna's relationship with Mademoiselle Reisz? Is it a positive relationship for Edna? What does the Mademoiselle reveal about Edna?

7. How do you see her relationship with Alcée Arobin?

8. Is Madame Ratignolle right to warn her about her behaviour and its consequences? Think also about her comments at the end of the childbirth scene. How do these affect Edna?

9. Do you like Doctor Mandalet as a character? Support your answer with specific reference to the text.

10. Some critics have suggested that Edna Pontellier does not commit suicide at the conclusion of the novel and Chopin leaves some uncertainty. How do you see the conclusion of the novel? Support your thoughts with ideas/ quotes from the text.

11. Why do you think Chopin called the novel The Awakening?

12. *The Awakening* was heavily criticised in its time. Can you see why some people may not like the novel? Do you think what Edna Pontellier does is correct? Think not just about her actions and their effect but also on the moral and ethical conventions of her society.

13. What is your opinion of The Awakening? Do you think it appeals to a modern, teenage audience?

14. Discuss why this novel is admired by feminists and has become more popular in recent decades. If you are interested in this aspect read the introduction and follow up on some of the further suggested reading included on pages 35 to 38 of *The Awakening* (Penguin Classic edition).

SETTING

The setting of *The Awakening* is based around the state of Louisiana and in particular the city of New Orleans and its surroundings. Louisiana is one of the southern states of North America and it has very specific French, Spanish, Native American, Haitian and African influences as it was originally a French colony named after King Louis XIV of France. The state has a sub-tropical climate and is situated on the Gulf of Mexico. This is relevant to the novel as Summer is hot and thus the wealthy can escape the city onto various islands in the Gulf.

The city of New Orleans is named after the Duke of Orleans and is often called the 'most unique city in the world' because of its mix of races and cultural diversity. It is known for its lifestyle of festivals and culture. It borders the Mississippi and is the largest city in Louisiana but not the capital which is Baton Rouge. Also relevant background information you may need is the use of the term Creole in the novel. Louisiana Creole people are descendants of the original colonial settlers and the term usually refers to the

Spanish, African and French settlers who are often characterised by their use of French and Catholicism. Thus we can see the background of the novel is important so now I will focus on the specific setting in the text.

The Awakening begins on the Lebrun family island, Grand Isle, where the main characters meet for the annual holidays and where Edna Pontellier discovers her ability to transform and become a free woman in the sense of how she feels about herself and what she can do. The island is also the place where she goes to finish her days of freedom by swimming out to sea until exhausted. The island is a place of comparative freedom. Here she is somewhat more out of the control of her husband. We read of the effect of Grand Isle on Edna,

> *'That summer at Grand Isle she began to loosen a little the mantle of reserve that had always enveloped her. There may have been - there must have been - influences, both subtle and apparent, working in their several ways to induce her to do this...' (p57)*

One of these factors is Adele Ratignolle but another is Robert Lebrun, the man she falls in love with. It is her desire for change that moves her to be an independent, passionate woman back in her more restrained environment. In New Orleans they lived at Esplanade Street in a 'charming home' which is further described,

> *'It was a large, double cottage, with a broad front veranda....the appointments were perfect after the conventional type...The cut glass, the silver, the heavy damask which daily appeared upon the table were the envy of many women whose husbands were less generous than Mr Pontellier.' (p99)*

Mr Pontellier was indeed a man who 'valued his possessions, chiefly because they were his'. He is one aspect of her life that Edna breaks from. We see her retreat from expectation and domesticity as soon as she arrives home and she begins to ignore her domestic duties in favour of going out and practising art. She shows her intentions are serious when she abandons her home and finds lodgings of her own in the 'pigeon-house' where she establishes a new home for herself free from any connection with her husband's money and influence. This home is important to her,

> *'The pigeon-house pleased her. It at once assumed the intimate character of a home, while she herself invested it with a charm which it reflected like a warm glow. There was with her a feeling of having descended in the social scale, with a corresponding sense of having risen in the spiritual.' (p151)*

This change of residence reflects her new found freedom as a woman and her ability to survive on her own, under her own resources. It is a true moment for her and she is pleased with her ability to be alone. The change also allows her freedom of movement and association which provides opportunity for her passions and an increasingly erotic, moral and ethical freedom. Certainly she begins to follow her instincts and impulses, yet as I stated earlier she goes back to Grand Isle to conclude her quest. It is finally here on the beach with the 'voice of the sea' calling her that she feels born again,

> *'How strange and awful it seemed to stand naked under the sky! how delicious! She felt like some new-born creature, opening its eyes in a familiar world that it had never known.' (p175)*

Edna Pontellier's story ends here with her feeling misunderstood by the man whom she loved, Robert. She is not a possession but a woman who strived to be, as Mademoiselle Reisz says, 'dates and defies'.

Setting can certainly assist us in understanding the discoveries that Edna Pontellier makes in her life and the changes that these discoveries allow. Edna's settings change as she grows and as she develops her own independence and self-confidence.

Setting Questions and Activities

- Discuss the role of Grand Isle in the change and development of Edna. What environmental characteristics might aid this change compared to her life in New Orleans?
- Research Louisiana. Analyse the elements of the state that allow Chopin to add colour and texture to the novel.
- Describe the house in Esplanade Street.
- What do we learn about Mr Pontellier from the description of the house on page ninety-nine?
- What does Edna's move to the pigeon-house say about her state of mind?
- Describe the pigeon-house using your own words and quotes from the text.
- Why does Edna return to Grand Isle for the final scenes of the novel? What does Grand Isle offer in this instance?

CHARACTER ANALYSIS

Edna Pontellier

Edna Pontellier's story is one of transformation, a path of discovery of self, discovery of identity and finding a place in the world through these factors and defying convention. She is awakened to her sensuality and creativity one summer on Grand Isle through her contact with Adele Ratignolle, her developing love for Robert Lebrun and the general atmosphere of freedom created. We see here Edna taken out of her usual domestic environment and set into an atmosphere of nature and the senses. From her early descriptions Edna doesn't appear to be the remarkable woman she becomes, with:

> *'eyes... quick and bright; they were a yellowish brown, about the color of her hair. She had a way of turning them swiftly... Her eyebrows were a shade darker than her hair...She was rather handsome than beautiful. Her face was captivating by reason of a certain frankness of expression and a contradictory subtle play of features. Her manner was engaging.' (p45-46)*

At this point Edna is still domestic in the sense that she values home and hearth but we see on the island that she begins to argue with her husband Leonce, and defy him in little ways she never had before. He senses her lack of domesticity in her behaviour toward the children and then in her subtle defiance all of which later become more obtuse. Edna's transition is also seen in her developing sensuality as she discovers her passions through a series of liaisons with Alcée Arobin and her longing for Robert Lebrun. These passions are not just sexual they are also manifested in her life and art.

Edna casts off her old life, moving home, leaving her children and husband and discovering new activities and friends. These passions are combined to some extent in the final dinner party she gives at the Esplanade Street residence before moving to the pigeon-house. The discoveries Edna makes on the way to her final swim allows her to become independent and self-sufficient. She tells Mademoiselle Reisz,

> *'I have a little money of my own...I won a large sum this winter on the races, and I am beginning to sell my sketches.' (p134)*

These changes in Edna also affect other characters. We will discuss Leonce Pontellier next but she also impacts those around her. Robert goes to Mexico to escape her charms and his attachment to her. She is engaging to Arobin and physically attractive; to Mademoiselle Reisz she is a companion while she becomes a concern to the Doctor and Madame Ratignolle. The breakout changes that she makes in her life are significant enough to impact those around her and engender strong feelings. She is warned by her friend, even to the extent that after giving birth Adele says to Edna,

> *'Think of the children, Edna. Oh think of the children! Remember them!' (p170)*

This direct appeal to her maternal instincts goes unrewarded as Edna has decided long ago that she is not the maternal type and is able to sacrifice much to ensure her own identity. Edna is not a 'mother woman' and her instincts are not developed in this area. She informs Robert she is not a 'possession' and,

> *'I give myself where I choose.' (p167)*

Chafing against the established norms of her time is emotionally and spiritually exhausting. Her affair with Arobin is also fraught with strain. Despite her discovering her passion and sensuality, and the push to conform as reinforced by Adele Ratignolle, all leave her faint and spent. She has sacrificed much for her freedom and when she discovers Robert has left forever she spends the night contemplating her future. We have already seen her fragility in the previous conversation with Doctor Mandalet. We see the 'incoherency of her thoughts' and the conflict she feels. Edna tells the Doctor that she wants 'to be let alone' and perhaps her suicide is the ultimate extension of this, the ultimate freedom she cannot obtain in her society.

Edna Pontellier is often seen by critics as an iconic figure in early literary feminism. While this may be an accurate reading and can help us understand her thinking in abandoning her children and staid domestic life it is not the main concern of our studies. We must focus on Edna and what she discovers in doing this. Here we need to think back to one of our initial ideas that discoveries may not always be positive. While Edna does make some positive discoveries and finds some liberation in her new life, it does have negative impacts on her and those close to her. In the end Edna's discoveries end in her death. While she has had glimpses of the life she yearns for, it is in vain. It many ways her story is a tragedy because her aspirations now seem so ordinary to us. Consider the context of her time and how she is constrained by her society. Perhaps this is one of the discoveries she allows us to see. We will examine this more in the themes section of this guide but now we will examine the impact her discoveries have on other characters.

Leonce Pontellier

Mr Pontellier is described as,

> *'a man of forty, of medium height and rather slender build; he stooped a little. His hair was brown and straight, parted on one side. His beard was neatly and closely trimmed.' (pp43–44)*

This description is telling in its ordinariness. He is a man whom Edna is not satisfied with despite his being a solid citizen, good provider and kind to her. We note early that he is aware of her inability to care for the children according to the standards of the day and he sees it as 'habitual neglect'. The other women at one point declare,

> *'Mr Pontellier was the best husband in the world.' (p50)*

and she has to agree, yet there is no love between them on her part. As she gradually withdraws from him and her domestic duties, he is puzzled and worried. We later learn the marriage,

> *'was purely an accident, in the respect resembling many other marriages which masquerade as the decrees of Fate...He fell in love...He pleased her; his absolute devotion flattered her. She fancied there was a sympathy of thought and taste between them, in which fancy she was mistaken.' (p62)*

In all ways, Mr Pontellier is a product of his time. He does not understand Edna at all. He is adept at business and managing affairs, comes from an established Creole family and is stable, all qualities that are traditionally admired. He knows the value of things and it is written,

'He greatly valued his possessions, chiefly because they were his, and derived genuine pleasure from contemplating...no matter what...after he had bought it and placed it amongst his household goods.' (p99)

This structure, order, routine or the fabric of his household is disturbed by Edna's change. He tries to ignore it, fix it and modify it and finally admits to Doctor Mandalet the problems are beyond his skills to identify and fix. He tells the Doctor,

'Her whole attitude - toward me and everybody and everything - has changed...making it devilishly uncomfortable for me...She's got some sort of notion in her head concerning the eternal rights of women...' (pp117-118)

The basic problem is that Leonce will never understand his wife and she never loves him in a passionate sense. He has a very particular sense of duty rather than a passionate life. This is not enough for Edna who wants to be an individual, not a possession. Leonce is all about perceptions. We see this in his covering up of her absence from taking visitors on Tuesdays and his newspaper excuse for her moving out of the home on The Esplanade. Leonce Pontellier is a solid, respected man and one who is not used to being defied. Edna eventually no longer exists in his world.

What you as a reader need to decide is whether he is portrayed sympathetically by Chopin or some other picture is shown. He is not cruel or unkind and his expectations of her are limited but understandable for the context. Edna is the focus but Leonce's world changes dramatically as she does and he doesn't comprehend the changes in any meaningful way. It is hard to see how her death might affect him but he never discovers the key to her happiness nor does he understand her unhappiness. It seems they are worlds apart without any hope of understanding each other. Leonce Pontellier is a man of his time.

Robert Lebrun

The Lebrun family run the guest houses on Grand Isle and every year Robert attaches himself to one of the women in a flirtatious manner until the year he becomes more than attached to Edna. With her, things become very different and he falls in love. In the past he knows the women are unattainable but his change is significant in that his attentions awaken in Edna part of that life missing in her marriage. In a sense, he is awakened to her and she to a new life. Robert is not a wealthy man. He is on Grand Isle to assist his mother run the cottages for the exclusive rich of New Orleans so his mother can make money from the old 'summer luxury' of her family. Robert has a,

'modest position in a mercantile house in New Orleans, where an equal familiarity with English, French and Spanish gave him no small value as a clerk and correspondent.' (p46)

He has intended to go to Mexico to further his ambitions but never quite makes the change. He is a man who 'talked a good deal about himself. He was a young man who didn't know any better' but Edna falls for him anyway because of his attentions. Robert is warned by Madame Ratignolle about his flirting with Edna but he tells her,

'I hope Mrs Pontellier does take me seriously. I hope she has discernment enough to find in me something more beside the blagueur. If I thought there was any doubt - ' (p64)

His attentions become so serious and overwhelming that he does go to Mexico to the shock of Edna yet she maintains an attachment to him through his mother and Mademoiselle Reisz. His mother shares some childhood memories of him through a photo or two, but there was 'no recent picture' to soothe the recognition in her that she missed him. It is on Robert's leaving that she realises that,

> *'she recognized anew the symptoms of infatuation which she had felt incipiently as a child, as a girl in her earliest teens, and later as a young woman.' (p94)*

Mademoiselle Reisz also notices her pain and she seems to understand Edna well. The best example of this is on page 95 where Chopin writes how well Reisz mirrors the feelings of Edna. Mademoiselle Reisz also enables Edna to keep up with Robert's whereabouts and progress through the letters she shares with Edna that have been sent by Robert. Robert's letters reveal something about his progress which isn't much but more about his relationship with Edna according to Reisz. She states that the letters include nothing about Edna and he has never written to her because,

> *'he loves you, poor fool, and is trying to forget you, since you are not free to listen to him or belong to him.' (p135)*

When Robert comes back he declares his undying love and she returns it with fervour and the reader thinks that things might play out like a fairy tale yet the context and the roles that are supposed to be played with honour don't allow this. Robert is gone when she returns from the birth of Madame Ratignolle's child and he has left a note,

> *'I love you. Good-by - because I love you,' (p172)*

Robert has gone and with it he takes Edna's desire to continue. The awakening she has had, the discovery of the glimpse of a new life, has been started by Robert and then abruptly taken away. Robert Lebrun is the catalyst for her change and also for her demise. Does he discover that he is too tied to tradition and social niceties or is a he just weak or both? He is charming and Edna falls for him so we must also acknowledge the positive qualities he has. Perhaps Robert is as complex as the woman he loves.

Adele Ratignolle

Adele Ratignolle is an archetypal 'mother-woman' the opposite of Edna and,

> *'There are no words to describe her save the old ones that have served so often to picture the bygone heroine of romance and the fair lady of our dreams. There was nothing subtle or hidden about her charms; her beauty was all there, flaming and apparent: the spun-gold hair that comb nor confining pin could restrain, the blue eyes that were like nothing but sapphires...' (p51)*

This description goes on for nearly the full page and Adele is a character whom Chopin wants us to heed. In many ways, she is the direct contrast to Edna in that she is the archetypal women and doesn't seek to break the pattern of the quintessential woman of the times. She is a dedicated and excellent mother and housewife, yet she also can tell a spicy story. She is always suffering from her 'condition' which is perpetual pregnancy as she has a baby every two years.

Adele Ratignolle is also aware and doesn't live her life with blinkers on despite her maternal manner. She warns Robert about fooling with Edna's affections and also warns Edna about the changes she is making to her life. Edna feels Adele's life is depressing,

'The little glimpse of domestic harmony...gave her no regret, no longing. It was not a condition of life which fitted her, and she could see in it but an appalling and hopeless ennui. She was moved by a kind of commiseration for Madame Ratignolle, - a pity for that colorless existence...' (p107)

Madame Ratignolle would not see her life like this and is quite content to love her husband and children. She warns Edna again just after the birth of her fourth child not to abandon her own two boys. The warning to think of the children is very typical of the thinking of the times and certainly in this context. Edna doesn't heed the advice at any point in her determination to forge a new life for herself but Adele is a good foil to show how far that Edna takes her life away from the norm. Adele is the nineteenth century's idea of the perfect woman and Edna rejects this for independence as illustrated by our next character, Mademoiselle Reisz.

Mademoiselle Reisz

Mademoiselle Reisz is Chopin's method of illustrating what Edna would have been had she not swum out into the Gulf. Reisz is Edna a few decades hence, an independent woman of independent means who is be holding to no-one or anything, especially a man. For most readers and indeed the characters in *The Awakening*, including Edna, the Mademoiselle is a disagreeable woman yet despite this Edna is drawn to her for want of a better word, reassurance.

The Mademoiselle is certainly able to manage on her own and is described as, *'a homely woman, with a small weazened face and body and eyes that glowed. She had absolutely no taste in dress, and wore a batch of rusty black lace with a bunch of artificial violets pinned to the side of her hair.' (p71)*

When they leave Grand Isle and head back to New Orleans Edna uses Reisz's home as a kind of refuge, to read the letters, to wallow in the piano music and to use the Mademoiselle as a sounding board. They become more than acquaintances and Reisz is invited to the final dinner at the old house. At this she leaves with the advice, 'Bonne nuit, ma reine; voyez sage' (Goodnight, my queen, be wise). This sums up their relationship, the older, wiser voice who admires but also cautions Edna. Mademoiselle Reisz is the fate of an independent woman in that context and as readers we need to decide if the sacrifices she has made to achieve that goal are balanced by what she is.

Other Characters

Alcée Arobin is Edna's lover and already has a scandalous reputation as we hear early from Madame Ratignolle and her story of Arobin 'and that story of the consul's wife at Biloxi. He is the 'comfort' that Edna enjoys while Robert and her husband are away. She thinks,

'Alcée Arobin was absolutely nothing to her. Yet his presence, his manners, the warmth of his glances, and above all the touch of his lips upon her hand had acted like a narcotic to her.' (p132)

For Edna, Alcée is a good time, at the house, at the races and in company. He awakens in her the sense of passion she didn't have in her marriage and allows her to explore this fully.

Victor Lebrun is another character who is at the final dinner party at the old house. He is 'the younger son and brother...with a temper which invited violence and a will which no axe could break.' (p67) He is a young man out for a good time and is able to continue to do this as it is acceptable for a male figure. He is there at the end of the novel basically to be shocked at Edna's reappearance at the island.

Mrs Lebrun is also an example of a woman changed after her husband's demise. She is used to living in some luxury in the big house and now has to take in the rich to support a lifestyle she had become used to.

Doctor Mandalet is an interesting character in that he is an observer without judgement. He listens to Mr Pontellier and offers advice, knowing Edna may be in love with another man and he listens to Edna and offers to help if she requires it. He is an example of a man who has seen and experienced much and is able to analyse the situation without bias. He tells her as they part for the last time,

> *'We will talk of things you never have dreamt of talking about before. It will do us both good. I don't want you to blame yourself, whatever comes. Good night, my child.' (p172)*

Perhaps Edna should have gone to see him.

Character Questions

- Describe the relationship between Edna and Leonce Pontellier.
- Why is Leonce so surprised by Edna's behaviour?
- Do you think that Robert Lebrun truly loves Edna? Support your ideas with specific evidence from the text.
- Analyse why Mademoiselle Reisz becomes a role-model of sorts for Edna. What qualities does she have that intrigue Edna?
- Discuss the role of the Ratignolle family in the novel. Think about why Chopin included them in the novel and for what purpose.
- Analyse how the passion and emotion in Edna is aroused throughout the novel. You may like to refer to this in terms of her journey of discovery. Comment on the character(s) who develop these aspects of her inner self.
- Discuss in detail the role of ONE minor character in the novel and their impact on Edna Pontellier in terms of her initiating/developing her new independent life in New Orleans.

THEMATIC CONCERNS

Discovery

While *The Awakening* is obviously about the awakening awareness in Edna it is also a journey of discovery, not just for Edna but for some of the other characters such as Robert and Mr Pontellier. It is easy to see that for some characters this sense of discovery is positive and for some negative while you can argue that for Edna it is both. It is also extremely important to remember the context of the novel and indeed the author. For a modern reader what Edna does may not be strange and even be accepted, but in the context of the times it was certainly radical and unique. While I do not adhere to some of the more wild feminist readings of this novel there can be no doubt that some of the ideas that Edna pursues are now basic feminist tenets but don't get caught up in this, remember the bigger picture which is all types of discovery.

We do need to examine the discoveries Edna makes on her journey to an independent life. Early in the novel she concludes that she is not a maternal woman in any sense and while there is an element of guilt over her leaving her children she seems able to compartmentalise this and move on. The first steps toward independence occur on Grand Isle when she discovers the passion that is missing in her marriage. We have already discussed how her marriage was never based on passion and her earlier loves were unrequited. Here on the Isle she finds Robert and he begins to rekindle these feelings. This discovery that she could again be infatuated is clearly delineated in the quote,

'The present alone was significant; was hers, to torture her as it was doing then with the biting conviction that she had lost that which she had held, that she had been denied that which her impassioned, newly awakened being demanded.' (p94)

This initial discovery that she could follow her passions leads her to revel in her own needs which have been previously supplanted by her denying these for other people and social convention. One example of this is her art which she begins to make her focus rather than the social visits she made and received. She,

'began to do as she liked and to feel as she liked. She completely abandoned her Tuesdays at home, and did not return the visits of those who had called upon her. She made no ineffectual efforts to conduct her household en bonne ménagère...' (p107)

These changes both 'bewilder' and 'anger' her husband who discovers a very new wife to the one he was used to. He leaves her alone as requested and develops strategies to control the situation, but he does wonder if she is not becoming a 'little mentally unbalanced'.

As Edna progresses in her discoveries, we see internal and external changes in her and also in the manner of her interactions with others and society. As she follows this path of self-discovery, unlocking the passionate side of herself her public persona changes. Some examples of this are her changing tastes in entertainment such as going to the races, the dinner party and the move to the 'pigeon house' which delineates a move from her past life to the present in a clear way. Here she also seems to break from her family, withdrawing from her children and her father and sister. It is clear that she is becoming self-reliant, moving away from all the restrictions of her previous existence.

One question that we must ask in reference to discovery is what we think Edna discovers about herself on the journey we just briefly examined. Certainly she becomes more confident in herself and her choices. She discovers new connections. Her sexuality is unleashed in an erotic manner and her view of the world is less rigid and conformist. If we, as modern readers, consider these to be positive traits then why does it all end tragically? Perhaps the discoveries that Edna makes are too much too soon. Perhaps she is eventually condemned by her new found love for Robert and his own personal struggle with social mores which drive him to leave despite his obvious love. To form your own ideas on these questions you need to focus on the final pages of the text and Edna's swim into the Gulf.

On this swim she thinks of her family and how they thought they could possess her, body and soul', Mademoiselle Reisz and 'the courageous soul that dares and defies', Robert who 'would never understand' and finally Doctor Mandalet who would 'have understood' had it now not been too late. Her final thoughts are back to her family childhood where she was happy and free before she was constrained. Edna's transformation is totally for herself and in many ways she is successful in finding what she wants. Certainly with Arobin she finds her sexuality,

> *'It was the first kiss of her life to which her nature had really responded. It was a flaming torch that kindled desire...But among the conflicting sensations which assailed her, there was neither shame nor remorse. There was a dull pang of regret because it was not the kiss of love which had inflamed her, because it was not love which had held this cup of life to her lips.' (p139)*

With Robert she finds love and tells him,

> *'I love you," she whispered, "only you; no one but you. It was you who woke me last summer out of a life-long stupid dream... I have suffered, suffered! Now you are here we shall love each other, my Robert.' (p168)*

Edna also finds her creativity through her art which she practises assiduously. It improves enough for her to sell works through Laidpore which provides some independence giving cash flow. Another focus point for her development is the business of being alone. While this seems to be a minor one Edna discovers her solitude, something she rarely had in married life. This ability to be alone gives her the time to investigate her motivations and her spirituality in terms of her place in the larger universe.

It is in the final action of that swim into the seducing sea where she feels reborn and free. Edna is finally able to connect, through her despondency, to a type of 'new-born' feeling. While this discovery is fleeting it is nonetheless important and childlike as she mentally harkens back to that 'blue-grass meadow' which had 'no beginning and no end.' Edna has discovered much about herself and others on this journey and her tragic conclusion can't diminish this.

One idea that I mentioned at the beginning of this discussion on discovery was that the discoveries Edna makes also lead to discoveries about other characters. Robert, for example, has his character drawn out by Edna's love. Robert, appears to be weaker than her despite,

> *'Her seductive voice, together with his great love for her, had enthralled his senses, had deprived him of every impulse but the longing to hold her and keep her.' (p168)*

Robert does leave. He has discovered his passion too, but is afraid and as she rightly thinks doesn't understand her. Robert seems a child of his time and social position. We already know that Leonce Pontellier has never understood her or her needs and in fact doesn't consider them. He knows she is not maternal and cannot ever come to terms with her discovering herself. He finds her 'peculiar' while Dr Mandalet surmises she might have been associating with 'pseudo-intellectual women - super spiritual superior beings.' Edna is a woman out of time in her context and perhaps the only way to express herself is in death. Certainly Robert's weakness is a comment on the social values of the times and the sway they had. We can think about what makes him decide to leave and his parting note that expresses love as his reason for leaving seems weak and ineffectual to a modern reader but perhaps less so if we consider the issue in context.

Part of Edna's discovery of and journey to independence is that other characters also discover things about themselves. We, as audience, are able to judge them on this, as I think we judge Edna. Being around Edna just confirms for Madame Ratignolle the importance of her family and she cannot understand Edna's attitude, yet she never abandons her. The Madame just reinforces the stereotypes of the age and the maternal view of women. She doesn't really need to discover anything and is quite content with her lot in life.

Perhaps the key discovery that Edna makes can be summed up in the quote,

> *'The years that are gone seem like dreams - if one might go on sleeping and dreaming - but to wake up and find - oh! well! perhaps it is better to wake up after all, even to suffer, rather than to remain a dupe to illusions all one's life.' (p171)*

She concludes here in her admission to Dr Mandalet that it is better to have lived a little than never to have lived at all. She breaks from social niceties in a way that Robert could never conceive of. This quote is probably the key to the novel and a synopsis of what Edna's journey of self–discovery entails.

One of the other aspects of her discoveries about life is the fact that they isolate her in so many ways. In the final days she is truly alone and the outcome of this is total independence, something that would seem she aspired to, yet it drives her to swim out into the water, never to return. Her independence is somewhat false and socially she is an outcast, especially after Robert abandons her for the social mores she rejects. This profound isolation is what marks the end of her days. It is not a positive discovery about life, and one she may not have foreseen despite the abandoning of her husband and children. Countering this bleak picture is that she discovers her creativity, both artistically and sexually. Both of these bring her much joy and through these she discovers much about herself. Chopin balances these but overtly criticises the society of the day for not being accepting or understanding of female individuality or expression.

Much like Edna, Chopin herself suffered for her art as this novel was rejected by critics and readers alike for being too sexual, too permissive in its content and anti-maternal. In the next section we will examine how the literary techniques used by Chopin helps us add to our understanding of discovery in the novel. Both Edna and Chopin are reminiscent of the broken birds that are used to symbolise the women in the novel.

Questions on Discovery

- Discuss ONE discovery that Edna makes in the novel. How does it affect her life? Support your ideas with evidence from the text.
- List five examples of discovery in the novel that we see through other characters. Try to explain your choices fully and support them with direct quotations from the text.
- Analyse the negative aspects of Edna's discoveries. Do you think she gains more than she loses if we ignore her death?
- Discuss the impact of Madame Ratignolle in the novel. Is she a contrast to Edna? Do you think she makes any discoveries in the context of the novel?
- Discuss the idea that the novel could be simply called *The Discovery* as Edna's awakening is so akin to discovering self?
- Edna's journey takes her from a position of belonging to one of isolation both socially and personally. Consider this proposition in the light of the context of the novel.

LANGUAGE

The natural style of the novel is also infused with a particular Southern style that permeates the characters and provides context. Chopin's third person style, although detached at times, also imbues the characterisation of Edna with a sense of sympathy throughout her journey of discovery. Much of the story is akin to a Bildungsroman i.e. a type of novel concerned with the education, development, and maturing of a young protagonist. In this case our protagonist is not so young but the path of discovery is just the same and Edna also learns and grows to self–knowledge.

The Southern style that gives the novel a real sense of place is not just the use of the French language and the Creole customs and ideas but the lifestyle of the people and the places they inhabit. We see the wealth and privilege that the wealthy have in their sheltered lives and the particular customs of New Orleans and Louisiana. It is a setting of expectation. As Edna awakens we see these expectations shattered, especially as Edna has a very particular position and role in that society. Her discovery of an independent life breaks this Southern social expectation and indeed societal expectation in general, especially her abandonment of the children and her husband.

In narrating this, Chopin uses particular motifs and symbols to convey her ideas on Edna and women in particular. She foreshadows events such as the leaving of the family with her early comments on her maternal instincts and her final swim is foreshadowed in her earlier swim. The children are a motif in themselves and continually recur as Edna struggles with her own emotions and values while in some ways being a child herself as she grows as a person. She loves the children but will not sacrifice her own life for them and we read,

> *'She was fond of her children in an uneven, impulsive way. She would sometimes gather them passionately to her heart; she would sometimes forget them...Their absence was a sort of relief...' (p63)*

This recurring motif of children is reinforced by the views of Madame Ratignolle but as we have discussed this earlier I want to move on to the motif of Edna as a child. Edna of course is like a child as she grows and learns about her new life. Chopin compares her to a child especially at the conclusion when she is compared to a 'new-born creature, opening its eyes in a familiar world that it had never known' (p175) and Chopin also has Edna reverting to a child as she goes through her final struggle in the water. Another motif that carries through the novel is that of houses.

The first housing we read of are the holiday cottages at the Lebrun house on Grand Isle. These cottages are all joined and the dining is in the old, large more formal house on the estate. It is here that Edna discovers what is important to her. Back in New Orleans the Pontellier's have a 'charming home' which is well appointed and a credit to her husband. It is a home fitting their position in society and it represents her confinement under his rule and societal expectation. The 'pigeon house' as it becomes known is hers and represents her new life. It 'pleased' her and:

> *'assumed the intimate character of a home, while she herself invested it with a charm which it reflected like a warm glow. There was with her a feeling of having descended in the social scale, with a corresponding sense of having risen in the spiritual.'(p151)*

This house is hers and hers alone and represents her sense of independence and freedom from convention and expectation. This sense of freedom is also conveyed in the symbol of the birds which links the different areas of her growth.

In the early section of the book we see the 'green and yellow parrot' with a 'mocking-bird that hung on the other side of the door, whistling its fluty notes out on the breeze with maddening persistence.' (p43) These birds are owned by Mrs Lebrun and are caged, controlled, confined just like Edna. Later we see the parrot removed as it squawks and is 'consigned to regions of darkness.' (p69) Further on Mademoiselle Reisz warns Edna of birds that soar while in her final moments Edna sees,

> *'A bird with a broken wing was beating the air above, reeling, fluttering, circling disabled down, down to the water.' (p175)*

This is Edna in many ways free yet unable to make the most of her freedom, a broken creature. We have already talked about the influence of the sea in the novel but as a technique it is worth again considering here. The sea is linked with her journey to confidence as she learns to handle the water and it signifies a change,

> *'A feeling of exultation overtook her, as if some power of significant import had been given her to control the working of her body and her soul. She grew daring and reckless, overestimating her strength. She wanted to swim far out, where no woman had swum before.' (p73)*

This event is foreshadowing her final swim. Look for the water motif and the bird motif as you read. Find other examples and apply them to your own ideas. One final idea I would like to engage you with is the idea of music as a force. I have already discussed the concept of creativity linked to independence but the music is one aspect of creativity and passion that is also important to Edna's development. We first see this at the Lebrun residence when Mademoiselle Reisz plays,

> *'But the very passions themselves were aroused within her soul, swaying it, lashing it, as the waves daily beat upon her splendid body. She trembled, she was choking, and the tears blinded her.' (p72)*

Another incident at Mademoiselle Reisz's brings a similar reaction,

> *'Edna was sobbing, just as she has wept one midnight at Grand Isle when strange, new voices awoke in her.' (p116)*

Music signifies the awakening passion and emotions in Edna's life and is a clear symbol of her changing life.

You can now see how Chopin uses a variety of techniques to convey her ideas, not just about discovery, but about her other concerns as well.

Questions on Language

- Do you think the story is accessible to the modern reader? Support your ideas with evidence from the text.
- List five examples of the use of French in the text. Why does Chopin use French at times in the text? What does it add to our understanding of the people and times?
- Analyse ONE motif in the novel in detail, using specific quotes from the text to support your ideas.
- Discuss the use of symbols in *The Awakening*. Do you think they are appropriate in the context of the novel?
- Find some examples of dialogue in the novel that show the type of discoveries that Edna is making. Do you think Chopin portrays Edna's changing persona well?
- How valuable is the use of description in the text? Choose ONE particular setting, place or person to support your ideas. What do you think Chopin's use of description adds to the novel and to the reader's understanding of the protagonist?

THE ESSAY

The essay has been the subject of numerous texts and you should have the basic form well in hand. The point teachers would emphasise would be to link the paragraphs both to each other and back to your argument (which should directly respond to the question). Of course ensure your argument is logical and sustained.

Make sure you use specific examples and that your quotes are accurate. To ensure that you respond to the question make sure you plan carefully and are sure what relevant point each paragraph is making. It is solid technique to actually 'tie up' each point by explicitly coming back to the question.

When composing an essay the basic conventions of the form are:

- State your argument, outline the points to be addressed and perhaps have a brief definition.

↓

A solid structure for each paragraph is:

- Topic sentence (*the main idea and its link to the previous paragraph/ argument*)
- Explanation/ discussion of the point including links between texts if applicable.
- Detailed evidence (*Close textual reference- quotes, incidents and technique discussion.*)
- Tie up by restating the point's relevance to argument/ question

↓

- Summary of points
- Final sentence that restates your argument

As well as this basic structure you will need to focus on:

Audience

For the essay the audience must be considered formal unless specifically stated otherwise. Therefore your language must reflect the audience. This gives you the opportunity to use the jargon and vocabulary that you have learnt in English. For the audience ensure your introduction is clear and has impact. Avoid slang or colloquial language including contractions (like doesn't, e.g., etc.).

Purpose

The purpose of the essay is to answer the question given. The examiner evaluates how well you can make an argument and understand the module's issues and its text(s). An essay is solidly structured so its composer can analyse ideas. This is where you earn marks. It does not retell the story or state the obvious.

Communication

Take a few minutes to plan the essay. If you rush into your answer it is almost certain you will not make the most of the brief 40 minutes to show all you know about the question. More likely you will include irrelevant details that do not gain you marks but waste your precious time. Remember an essay is formal so do not do the following: story-tell, list and number points, misquote, use slang or colloquial language, be vague, use non sentences or fail to address the question.

PLAN: Don't even think about starting without one!

Introduce...

the texts you are using in the response

Argument: That discovery is affected by:

- A sense of place
- People you meet
- Context and environment

You need to let the marker know what texts you are discussing. You can start with a definition but it could can come in the first paragraph of the body. You MUST state your argument in response to the question and the points you will cover as part of it. Don't wait until the end of the response to give it!

↓

Idea 1 – Discovery comes from the place where it is new and exciting.

Idea 2-People's ideas about discovery are affected by other people

- explain the idea
- where and how shown in prescribed text?
- where and how shown in related text 1?
- where and how shown in related text 2?

Idea 3- People's sense of discovery is affected by context and environment

- explain the idea
- where and how shown in prescribed text?
- where and how shown in related text 1?
- where and how shown in related text 2?

You can use the things you have learned to organise the essay. For each one you say where you saw this in your prescribed text and where in related text(s).

Two or three ideas are usually enough as you can explore them in detail.

↓

- Summary of two key ideas
- Final sentence that restates your argument

Make sure your conclusion restates your argument. It does not have to be too long.

MODEL ESSAY OUTLINE

> *To what extent is discovery important?*
>
> *From your studies respond to this question using your set text and at least two pieces of other textual material*

This essay needs to be attacked in a manner that responds to the question and shows ALL your knowledge about the text. The question lends itself to a close study of *The Awakening* as the text does show how discovery is important to our psyche and how it is part of life.

A beginning to a more complex introduction might be written:

Discovery is important in *The Awakening* and the two related texts Janis Ian's *At Eighteen* and Levine's film *50/50*. These texts show how discovery and the path to and from discovery can change the world, groups of people and individuals. Discovery is about possibility, change and the benefits and disadvantages that accrue from its pursuit.

Your essay should then follow an outlined plan and develop these ideas. This gives you the opportunity to link the texts and fully develop each of the ideas.

DISCOVERY: OTHER RELATED TEXTS

PROSE FICTION

Bypass – The Story of a Road by Michael McGirr

About one man's journey of discovery along the Hume Highway between Sydney and Melbourne.

Gulliver's Travels by Jonathan Swift

This classic tale is about Gulliver's discovery of Lilliput and through his arduous adventures he discovers lessons about society and humanity. The tale is a satirical view of the state of European government, and of petty differences between religions; as well as the origins of human corruption, the conflict between Lilliputians and Yahoos, and other races.

A History of Reading by Alberto Manguel

Discover a personal response to books and reading and a love of literature. Wonderful text.

Looking for Alibrandi by Melina Marchetta

The aspect of discovery here is Alibrandi discovering who her estranged father is, as well as coping with various teenage issues in high school.

Memoirs of a Geisha by Arthur Golden

This novel is about discovering who she is, developing her sense of identity in a tumultuous period in Japanese history.

***The Secret River* by Kate Grenville**

Discover the interaction between the white settlers and the Aboriginal population on the Hawkesbury River. Discovery about the journey, people and cultures.

***Small Island* by Andrea Levy**

Told by four narrators the novel is set during the Second World War and tells the story of four different lives. There is racial tension and discovery of what it is like living with someone who comes from a different part of the world. Not only do you discover this new way of life, but it brings about a discovery of the self.

***So Much To Tell You* by John Marsden**

Here a scarred and introverted girl discovers a way to reveal her feelings to the reader in the form of a diary. In turn, readers discover Marina's life and relationships as she also discovers non-verbal ways to communicate with others.

***Unpolished Gem* by Alice Pung**

Discovery between cultures and people in Footscray, Victoria. About discovering life in a family and about cultures.

***An Unsuitable Job for a Woman* by P.D. James**

Female detective Cordelia Gray investigates a suicide and a family with many secrets. Detailed writing with plenty of atmosphere and clues. Detection discovery with a twist.

***The Snowman* by Jo Nesbo**

Detective discovery in a European setting. Modern take on the genre and very well written.

FICTION / FILM

***Alice in Wonderland* (novel and film) original by Lewis Carroll**

Alice discovers a magical fantasy world where she is in turmoil. Here she has amazing adventures and meets many intriguing characters.

***Chronicles of Narnia* (novel and film) original by C.S. Lewis**

Four children, Peter, Suzan, Edmund and Lucy, discover a magical world behind their wardrobe and learn about their special role in saving the land from a great evil.

***The Lost Thing* (picture book and film) original by Shaun Tan**

A boy discovers a lost thing and journeys to find it a home.

***The Never-ending Story* (novel and film) original by Michael Ende**

The protagonist Sebastian discovers the world of Fantasia which is dying. He becomes part of the book he is reading and saves the world.

***Sherlock Holmes* (novel and film) original by Conan Doyle**

Any of the *Sherlock Holmes* mysteries of adventures such as *The Hound of the Baskervilles*. We are presented with discovery through means of deduction, calculation and scientific reasoning.

Under the Dome by Stephen King (novel and film)

Imagine being trapped and cut off from the world under a dome of power. Science fiction text that is a long read but intriguing idea. The initial discovery is awesome but then characters begin to discover things about themselves and others.

Where the Wild Things Are (picture book and film) original by Maurice Sendak

A young boy is punished by his mother to go to his bedroom, which transforms into a jungle where he sails to an island and discovers that it is inhabited by malicious beasts known as the "Wild Things." After successfully intimidating the creatures, Max is hailed as the king of the Wild Things and enjoys a playful romp with his subjects. However he discovers that being king is not all that great.

Wizard of Oz (novel and film) original by Frank L. Baum

Dorothy discovers a magical fantasy world where various characters discover their true character such as Tin Man finds his heart.

FILM

The Book Thief by Marcus Zusak

A young orphaned girl meets her new family in Germany during the Second World War. Through the focalisation of this young girl the reader pieces together the narration and discovers what is going on in the world around her. Historical discovery.

The Island directed by Michael Bay

Science fiction film about clones that live in a false utopian prison who discover their true origins as spare organ parts for wealth but terminally ill people. The revelation is the discovery and how the discoverers respond to it.

It's Kind of a Funny Story directed by Ryan Fleck

A teenage boy checks himself into the mental ward only to find he has been relocated to the adult's ward. The film follows the boy and the friends he makes along the way.

50/50 directed by Johnathon Levine

Adam learns how to cope and live his life by coming to terms with his cancer.

An Education directed by Lone Sherfig

Jenny is in her final year of high school and has high hopes for the future when she meets a middle aged man who shows her another world. Jenny has to decide which world she wants to live in.

POETRY

Easy Does It by Bruce Dawe

A poem about discovering his boy and how he has to be 'careful' with him.

Discovery by Wislawa Szymborksa

The poem begins with 'I believe in the great discovery' and it is about faith and evidence.

La Belle Dame Sans Merci by John Keats

A knight discovers a new love and a new faery world but it is not what it seems and his discovery in this poem leads him to a life of misery.

SONGS

At Seventeen by Janis Ian

Teen coming of age song about the angst of discovering what and who you are.

Kings and Queens by 30 Seconds to Mars

Discovering empowerment and greatness from despair.

Meant to Live by Switchfoot

Making the most out of life and discovering your absolute potential.

We Won't get Fooled Again by The Who

The persona in the song discovers that the new government which established after a revolution is the same as the old government, and criticises it.

WEBSITES

100 Questions to Inspire Self-Discovery

HTTP://WWW.ALEXANDRAFRANZEN.COM/2013/04/18/100-QUESTIONS-TO-INSPIRE-RAPID-SELF-DISCOVERY/

Quite a few sites like this one that offer ideas on the topic. Read judiciously.

Discover the Extreme World

HTTP://WWW.MILESKELLY.NET/PRODUCTS-PAGE/DISCOVERY-EXPLORE-YOUR-WORLD/

Read the book blurb: Produced in association with Discovery Channel, this jam-packed book focuses on the extremes of core reference subjects. From animal giants to futuristic spy technology to the deepest caves and coldest places in the Universe. Nice change as it is aimed at children.

Discover Magazine

HTTP://AU.ZINIO.COM/MAGAZINE/DISCOVER/PR-500621662

Science based but has a wide range of articles on all sorts of interesting topics such as foods and environment.

HTTP://WWW.MILESKELLY.NET/PRODUCTS-PAGE/DISCOVERY-EXPLORE-YOUR-WORLD/

Discovery channel

HTTP://WWW.DISCOVERYCHANNEL.COM.AU/

Here you will discover many shows about discovery but it is also about learning.

Discovery Education

HTTP://WWW.DISCOVERYEDUCATION.COM/TEACHERS/

This address will lead you to the teacher resources but the site is full of content that shows another aspect of discovery i.e. education.

Famous People who Made Scientific Discoveries

HTTP://WWW.BIOGRAPHY.COM/PEOPLE/GROUPS/DISCOVERY/SCIENTIFIC

Another excellent source for evidence in film and written form on a comprehensive site.

Kids Discover

iPad app. Below is the address for the preview but you can download the app and use it. Excellent resource.

HTTPS://ITUNES.APPLE.COM/AU/APP/KIDS-DISCOVER/ID574832964?MT=8

The Science Channel

SCIENCE.DISCOVERY.COM/FAMOUS-SCIENTISTS-DISCOVERIES/100-GREATEST-DISCOVERIES.HTM

Almost complete collection of all the scientific discoveries covering most of the ancient and modern worlds in film and clearly explained.

Self Discovery

HTTP://EN.WIKIPEDIA.ORG/WIKI/JOURNEY_OF_SELF-DISCOVERY

Here are some definitions and links to the topic. A useful starting point to develop your ideas.